C000049115

Eunice Chapman was born on the ███████ ████ ███ ███████ ██ a nurse in the 1950s, and settled ███ ███████ ██ ██████ ██████ years she helped run her husband's restaurant in Salcombe, before she met John Allen. More recently she has worked as a sub-editor on *Nursing Times*, but has now returned to Devon to write.

Presumed Dead

The True Story Of An Unsolved Mystery

An Autobiography
EUNICE CHAPMAN

WARNER BOOKS

A *Warner* Book

First published in Great Britain in 1992
by Warner Books
Reprinted 1993 (twice)

Copyright © 1992 by Eunice Chapman

The moral right of the author has been asserted.

A CIP catalogue record for this book is
available from the British Library
ISBN 0 7515 0774 1

Typeset in Galliard by Leaper & Gard Ltd, Bristol, England
Printed in England by Clays Ltd, St Ives plc

Warner Books
A Division of
Little, Brown and Company (UK) Limited
165 Great Dover Street
London SE1 4YA

Contents

Foreword:
A Country Mystery

If it is possible that a place can play a part in shaping events, not just because of its physical layout but because of its unchartable nature, then Salcombe could be said to be a leading character in this story.

It lies not on the open, rugged coast of South Devon, but tucked snugly inside a great inlet of the sea, known by yachtsmen and lovers of the town as Salcombe Estuary and by the inhabitants of Kingsbridge, the market town at its head, six miles to the north, as Kingsbridge Estuary. No river empties into it; it is in fact, not an estuary at all, but a ria, or series of drowned valleys. A vast expanse of sea water runs inland, branching into creeks in every direction, reflecting the green of the wooded slopes that rise steeply on all sides. It is extravagantly beautiful.

Life in a small seaside town differs from city life in that it is slower and people take a closer interest in the affairs of their neighbours because, generally, they know them better and for longer. Street for street, deception, desertion and adultery are probably no more prevalent than elsewhere, but they are more noticeable because there are fewer distractions. They raise eyebrows and lead to ribald comment in the pubs, but are usually soon forgotten.

Tourism is a major industry, benefiting the whole area, except perhaps the large population of retired people who endure the yearly influx of summer visitors with gritted teeth.

Some local people, who must be distinguished from those who merely live there, or those who own summer homes, still earn their livings from boat building and fishing, mainly for crabs and lobsters. The boats are mostly made of fibreglass now, and the crabbers pack their catch into refrigerated lorries to be transported to London, France and Spain, though they still supply the good-class hotels and restaurants. Newcomers are made welcome, but they can never cross the dividing line and become local, however long they remain.

The Allen family were newcomers. They arrived in 1974, when John took up his new appointment as restaurant manager at the three-star Marine Hotel. They were an attractive couple making a fresh start. John, a strong, good-looking man of forty, was not long out of prison, his earlier career having culminated in a three-year sentence for bigamy and fraud. Pat, blonde, pretty and a year younger, was his second wife. He had deserted his first, Monica, and their two small sons in dramatic circumstances. These things were not generally known, but were rumoured.

Pat was happy with the move. The flat provided by the Marine was pleasant and roomy, with views of the estuary. Little Vicky and Jonathan settled well into the infants' school and she began to look for a part-time job. Life promised to be better. John, secure in his new job, realised a long-held ambition and made a down payment on a second-hand cabin cruiser for family outings and fishing trips. It was tiny and inferior by Salcombe standards, but it was destined to acquire some significance.

Charles Yabsley was a true local, which is to say he was born in Salcombe, into a family with a local name that had lived in and around it for countless generations. He grew up at Beadon, his father's farm at the edge of the town, the fifth of seven children.

He was still living in the farmhouse with his mother and

younger sister when he was thirty-six. In fact, for the whole of his life, he made his home in Beadon valley, though his long service with the Royal Navy had taken him to every part of the world. When he came out, much decorated, he looked for a means of earning a living in Salcombe and opened what became a fashionable and, in its day, quite famous restaurant, the Galley.

He was more than simply popular with the townspeople; they actually loved him. A small man, with a wide engaging grin, he radiated warmth and joy in living. He was also well known as a county councillor with a genuine concern for his constituents. When he died suddenly at fifty-four of a coronary thrombosis, they were stunned. After his death there was a tremendous outpouring of goodwill. Letters, flowers and gifts showered on me, his wife Eunice.

I was fifteen years younger than Charles, or Charlie as everyone but his immediate family called him, and we had been married for eighteen years when he died. I had always worked in the restaurant, even when our three children were babies, sometimes running the bar and, when Charlie allowed or rather refrained from interfering, keeping the books and paying the bills. At the height of the summer season, I relieved him on three nights a week, managing the floor of the house; greeting the customers, taking orders, seeing that people were seated in turn and kept happy while they waited for a table. It was a demanding job, made more difficult because I had to contend with the disappointment of clients when they found they had come on Charlie's night off.

When he died, as well as the usual dilemma of how to care for the children while earning the money to feed them, I had other problems.

The Galley had accumulated massive debts. Charlie always managed to trade his way out of trouble in the summer when cash poured in, only to lose the ground he gained in the winter. The winter 1974 to 1975 was worse than usual. For much of the previous summer, the restaurant had been closed for rebuilding after a devastating fire: regrettably, it had been under-insured.

There were two options. Sell the Galley, find what work I could and get help from the state; or sell our home, Hangar Mill, pay the debts and carry on with the restaurant.

The house itself was in good repair, having been re-roofed and extended at a time when Charlie had dreamed of branching into the hotel business. The adjoining mill was derelict and the range of barns was falling into ruin. Money needed to be spent on them.

I could not really see myself in the role of destitute widow and I had bigger hopes for my children than simply seeing them well-fed. I had always worked without pay in the restaurant, thinking it was the best way of helping the family. For a couple of years, though, when cash had flowed in I had been able to find money to pay the children's school fees. Catherine, the eldest, was in her second year at a private school.

I would have left her at the local comprehensive school had she been happy and doing well, but she had been miserable. Now, twelve-year-old Stephen was under-achieving. Lorna, the little one, had ambitions to be a dancer. I meant to give them what chance I could. Having no natural leanings towards the restaurant business, I would not normally have chosen it, but in these circumstances, it had effectively chosen me. It was heartbreaking, but Hangar Mill had to go.

Help came from every quarter. My neighbours who owned the bakery next to the Galley offered me the flat above their shop. By cutting a doorway between the two buildings and bringing in the storerooms above the restaurant, I gained enough room to house us all and the dog and the two Siamese cats.

The sale of Hangar realised enough to pay all the debts with a little left over. For the first time since I married Charlie, I was in control of my own affairs and had money in the bank. It gave me a heady sense of freedom. Despite strong opposition from the family solicitor, who had been appointed by Charles to execute his will and whose duty it was to see the estate properly wound up, I set about running the Galley.

John and I met for the first time when he walked into the Galley late one night in the middle of February 1975, about three weeks after Charlie's death. He aroused my interest from the first. He took to calling in regularly, usually on a Thursday, after he finished work, to have a drink before going home. We had things in common; we both once lived in Basildon; we had both owned vintage MGs; and we both now owned basset-hound bitches, mine called Lucy, his called Fleur.

The Galley, having a licence to open late, closed long after the Marine. In the winter, the last customers were usually sitting by about 10.30pm but were allowed to go on drinking until 1am. I liked this time of the evening, and usually settled in the bar with the *Daily Telegraph* crossword. John began bringing in *The Times* and we worked together to finish them both. Sometimes he stayed on after the last customer had gone. By the end of April, he was staying the night.

John never spoke ill of Pat. He told me that when he first met her, he loved her so much, just looking at her brought a lump to his throat. She had been a loving wife, sticking to him through difficult times, but a coldness had been growing between them. They had tried to revive their old feelings, but the best they had managed was a polite co-existence. She still made him laugh at times, he said, but it seemed that even the new start in Salcombe was not going to bring them together. His job meant she spent most evenings alone and he thought she was getting phone calls from another man.

During those first weeks of widowhood, I had been driving my mother every afternoon to the cottage hospital in Kingsbridge, to visit my father who was terminally ill. It meant I had to give up the only time in the day when I should have been getting to grips with those details of business which make the difference between profit and loss: for example, how to make sure the staff didn't eat too much of the food, the wage levels to set and the proper pricing of drinks and food. This was worrying and I felt guilty that I should begrudge the time and, because the house was being sold, I couldn't bring my father home to die.

My parents Harry and Lil had followed me to Salcombe soon after I married. My father found work as a welder in Newton Abbot and my mother worked for Charlie, preparing vegetables in the restaurant kitchen, where she kept a sharp eye on his interests. They lived with us for a while, then moved around various rented flats until, when they reached retirement, they had been offered a flat, purpose built for elderly people by the council.

My father, Harry Chapman, had suffered angina for a number of years, but the shock of Charlie's sudden death, coupled with his anxiety about my predicament, brought on a stroke and a coronary thrombosis simultaneously, three days after the funeral.

My mother and I leaned heavily on each other through what was a testing time for us both. Lil was devastated by Harry's illness as he had been the pivotal point of her existence for more than fifty years but bore her trouble stoically. She never refused to help with the children or failed to turn up for work in the Galley kitchen. For my part, I was more in need of this kind of practical help than spiritual support. My apparent lack of sorrow over my bereavement had already caused comment, but I could not pretend to an emotion I did not feel.

Father lingered for four months and died on 21 May 1975. His burial had to take place on Friday, two days after he died, earlier than the family wished, because the following weekend was Spring Bank Holiday and no undertakers were working. Only half-a-dozen people were at that funeral, a sharp contrast to the occasion four months before, when the crowd assembled to honour Charlie's passing had filled Salcombe's huge Methodist church and overflowed into the surrounding streets.

On 24 May, the day after my father's funeral and the Saturday of the holiday weekend, John came to the Galley at about 11.30pm to see me. He wanted urgently to talk. I was standing by the open front door turning people away. It was a hot night and the place was packed. Conversation was impossible in the smoky crush, so, with some misgiving, I handed over to Judy, who assisted me, and walked with him to the gardens at the end of the street. We sat looking at the moonlit estuary and he told me Pat was threatening to leave him for her lover. He needed to know if I would look after Jonathan and Vicky if she left.

I was very aware that neither my own bereaved children nor the Galley were getting the amount of attention from me that they needed. It was less than a week since my gentle father had died and I had had no time to shed tears for him. Driven by the demands of the restaurant I'd gone to work on the night he died and on the night of his burial, containing my grief as best I could. I just couldn't face more demands on me. I was at the end of my strength and, in any case, I didn't believe Pat would leave her children. Few mothers do.

I'd never considered the possibility of setting up home with John, though I was by now deeply in love and was sustained by his love. It was difficult to refuse him anything, but adding to the burden of responsibility that I already carried was out of the question. I said 'No.'

Two days later, on 26 May, Spring Bank Holiday Monday, Pat Allen took Jonathan and Vicky, then aged six and five, to the fete in Malborough, a village three miles inland from Salcombe.

It was the last time anyone, apart from John, remembers seeing her.

On the next day, Tuesday, he arrived early in my flat, with

Vicky and Jonathan, small and bewildered, trotting at his heels. He seemed upset, but in control, drawing deep and fast on a cigarette. Pat and he had had a blazing row and she had gone, driving away in her ancient Volkswagen Beetle. Could the children stay with me while he did his morning shift, after which he would arrange for someone to look after them? Catherine, then not quite fifteen, took charge of them for the morning, taking them for a walk to Batson Creek to see the boats. In the afternoon, when lunch-time service finished at the Marine, John came back and he and I took Vicky, Jonathan and my ten-year-old Lorna to the beach at Thurlestone, driving the five miles or so in my new Volkswagen Golf, returning at about five-thirty, in time for me to open at seven.

To solve his baby-sitting problem, John swapped an evening session with a colleague. I got away as soon as I could and went to his flat in Powderham Villa. It was about 10.30pm and the children were in bed. Vicky was awake and crying with earache. Jonathan did not appear, apparently sleeping through his sister's wailing. John went upstairs to try to settle her but eventually carried her down to the living room. I held her in my lap while he rummaged through a plastic tub full of medicines and patent remedies, for some ear drops. He found them and while I held her, he put some in her ear. Once she was comforted, he carried her back to bed.

We sat together for a while and he asked if he could borrow my car the next day. His mother was coming from Bournemouth to take care of the children and he wanted to meet her at Totnes. Pat had taken the Beetle. I gave him the keys and left to get back to my own kids before the staff went home.

Neither of the Allen children was seen again.

I didn't see John at all that next day. When he returned my car keys on the day after, he told me he and his mother had talked things over and decided it would be best if she took the children back to Bournemouth. Later, he told me they were living with an aunt. I asked him a week or so later if he didn't want to see them and if he missed them. He replied he was sure it was better for them if he kept away. He did miss them. He thought he saw them everywhere, on the beach and in the street. In the face of such obvious pain, the subject was dropped. The children were seldom mentioned after that.

A year later, his mother was to deny that she had come to collect them. Nor was an aunt looking after them. Those aunts that he had were too old to take on the care of two small children.

After that eventful Bank Holiday weekend, we began to be more open about our relationship. We spent the day after he parted from the children together, with my sister who was still on a visit for my father's funeral. He seemed relaxed, almost carefree.

On most afternoons after that, I went to his flat. At night we slept in the single bed in my tiny room. He would hang behind when the last customers were leaving, then help with the rituals of locking up and putting the takings in the safe. Before daylight, he crept out so the children would not find us in bed together.

Pat left a good many possessions behind, including her passport, some of the children's clothing and several pieces of jewellery. The clothes may have been outgrown and the jewellery she may have rejected because she no longer loved the man who gave it to her. It is also possible that she had another passport, or that she felt she had no need of one. The clothes John gave away and the jewellery he offered to me, but I didn't want it. I put him in touch with old Percy Diamond.

Percy was on one of his annual visits to the Salcombe Hotel, which in its heyday had been a resort of the racing fraternity. A frequenter of race-tracks, Percy dealt in second-hand jewellery and went about with it stuffed in his pockets, loving the stir he caused when he produced charms from his waistcoat and bracelets from his trousers.

He looked at Pat's jewellery and paid for the items that interested him. The rest, a couple of long gold chains, a ring and a St Christopher medallion, were locked in the Galley safe and later handed to the police.

One evening towards the end of June, John appeared in the Galley with his dinner jacket over his arm. He had, he claimed, been given an ultimatum by the owner of the Marine Hotel to either give up seeing me or lose his job. His association with the proprietor of a rival, prestigious restaurant could not be tolerated. Undivided loyalty was demanded.

John chose to forfeit the job and with it the flat. He didn't stay to work out his notice, but left immediately. He was given two weeks to quit the flat.

I had been resisting pressure from him to allow him to move in with me, but I was now left without a choice. A partition was put up in one of the storerooms to make a double bedroom and John spent the last of his money on a lace-trimmed four-poster bed. The furniture in his flat belonged to the Marine Hotel. His personal belongings were packed into suitcases and my son's school trunk.

The season was building to its peak, so finding work for another pair of skilled hands was no problem. It was always a headache finding enough people to staff the place. On his first night, John found himself running the bar unaided. He had a pleasant, easygoing manner and was good at the job, though his bulk was a drawback in the restricted space. After a while, he joined me on the busiest nights, out on the restaurant floor, taking orders and serving wine.

Gradually, much of the day-to-day running fell to him. He began keeping the books, ordering the food and wine and paying the wages. I still did the hiring and housekeeping and paid the bills. It was unremitting toil for us both, but we worked well together.

It may or may not have been out of resentment at having a

new manager above him, but the chef gave notice a couple of weeks into the new arrangement, a severe blow in the middle of summer. If the waitresses and kitchen staff were put out, they didn't say so and in a short time they settled down and accepted the situation.

We were so wrapped up in each other, that the talk that was rumbling round the town didn't reach our ears, or if John knew of it, he paid no attention to it. My mother was hurt and offended by my living in sin, but she made no attempt at this stage to interfere. The hostility of Charles' relatives was something I regretted but had to accept as inevitable. Hardest to bear was Catherine's increasing alienation, but by then, I couldn't change anything. The moment when I might have changed the course of events had passed when I first let him kiss me. I could have discouraged him, but I chose not to; I could not have foreseen that this would bring down what seemed at times like the wrath of God. If I'd been more in control, I would have timed things differently.

If it had not all happened with such indecent speed; if my being widowed and meeting a new love could have been spread over three years instead of three months, Pat's leaving and our affair would have been of no more than passing interest. As it was, coming so soon after the death of their beloved Charlie, the people of Salcombe were shocked.

The rapidity with which events had followed one another and the number of suspicious circumstances raised a scandal that shook the small community. One of Pat's few remaining relatives, a distant cousin, came asking after her and gossip in the town reached such proportions that the police decided to act. A little less than a year after Pat and her children were last seen, Detective Chief Superintendent John Bissett, of Devon and Cornwall CID, launched the biggest missing-persons inquiry the nation has ever seen.

1

Angel by Name

At the end of June 1934, pretty Kitty Angel carried her long-awaited son Anthony John home to the Avenue in Bournemouth from a Devon nursing home. This had been her fourth pregnancy, but the first to have a successful outcome. The baby was long-limbed like his father but had his mother's slanted, rather cat-like eyes. His lack of brothers and sisters was compensated for by an abundance of cousins and aunts.

Kitty's mother had been one of identical twins, daughters of the leader of the Bournemouth Symphony Orchestra. Both girls had married Bournemouth men and produced large broods of children, all resembling each other and all brought up in close proximity. Most of the offspring were musical and had leanings towards the stage.

One of Kitty's younger female cousins almost made it to fame and fortune, appearing in 'Chu Chin Chow' and other major London musicals of the day, either in the chorus or as understudy to the leading singer. Her family were proud of her, seeing her as the epitome of all that is desirable in a woman: pretty, coquettish and manipulative. She fulfilled their predictions by marrying a man rich enough to provide her with real jewellery, a grand piano and a smart villa in Pinner where, when she was resting from the stage, she gave piano and elocution lessons.

Kitty much admired her and modelled her own life as closely as possible on hers, striving for perfection in all things, though the furnishings and cocktail parties at the house in Pinner could not be matched by those in the house on the Avenue. There was only one residential road in Bournemouth called a street and the Angels would not have considered living there.

Little Tony confounded his adoring mother by displaying a strong will and food-faddishness. So anxious was she that he should be properly nourished that when he refused her bread and butter pudding or bunny rabbit blancmange, she would place the bowl on the seat of a chair and make a game of spoon-feeding him through the bars at the back. Fascinated by the sight of his kneeling mother, he would eat every scrap.

Getting him to nursery school was a nightmare. He trotted docilely beside her until they reached the entrance porch, when he balked and utterly refused to go in. It was weeks before he could be persuaded to cross the threshold and years before he developed sufficient vocabulary to explain that he was too terrified to pass beneath the long icicle that hung from the fractured gutter.

With his scrubbed knees and short haircut, he grew up to be as wholesomely lower-middle class as an Ovaltine ad. At nine, he was sent to prep school in Wimborne, where he was judged to be very bright but lacking in perseverance. He did not complete his primary education there, but went home again to attend the local school and, after the 11-plus, grammar school.

He had his mother's word for it that his father adored him, but saw little sign of it. Jack Angel, retired from a British cavalry regiment, believed in strong discipline. Pleasures had to be earned and misdemeanours were punished by beatings.

On Saturday mornings, in common with the rest of Britain's child population, he went to the pictures and bought the *Beano*, but first he had to earn the money by cleaning his bicycle and his father's car.

His only fond memory of the father he feared was his

method of dispatching guests who overstayed their welcome, by looking pointedly at his watch, wandering into the hall to wind the long-case clock and returning bearing the visitors' outer clothing.

Both parents were keenly aware of the dangers inherent in his being an only child and tried to counteract any tendency to selfishness by insisting on perfect politeness and that he share his possessions.

He grasped the notion that there were advantages in having good manners but sharing never seemed such a good idea and its enforcement in early childhood had the effect of making him a secret hoarder, who in later life would lock a bread pudding in a safe to ensure that he had it all to himself.

By fifteen he had almost reached his full height of six foot and was ready for his first romantic encounter. He invited a girl he had been eyeing on the bus ride to school to spend a day on the beach. His mother packed a proper picnic basket for them, with napkins and china. The girl wore a black two-piece bathing suit. He was mesmerised by the red lines scoring her shoulders, due to the weight on her bra straps of her voluminous breasts. The sight of her scooping a blob of raspberry jam from where it had dropped into her cleavage, obliged him to spend much of his day lying face-down in the sand.

At seventeen and two weeks, he passed his driving test in his father's Rover. He was a member of the tennis club and played cricket regularly. For both sports, he was perfectly equipped, down to the right bag for carrying the gear. His uncle had got him articled to an architect whose office was within walking distance of the Avenue. It meant he could pop home for lunch.

Height and breadth of shoulders plus social polish were no doubt influential in getting him accepted on to an army-officer training course, after he decided a career in architecture was not for him. The Bournemouth *Evening Echo* carried a picture and a report of his being the first young man to enter the army under the new scheme, which Kitty cut out and pasted into her photograph album.

It wasn't any lack of ability or intelligence that caused him in the end to be rejected as officer material, but rather some unsuitable character trait; some unwillingness to conform. Either he didn't understand the reasons for his aspirations being blighted or he found them too difficult to face, but he could not explain it.

He stayed in the army, serving as a sergeant. Before his posting to Cyprus in 1956, at the height of that island's struggles to rid itself of British influence, he married Monica and took her with him to begin their lives together in married quarters on the army base.

Monica got secretarial work as part of the army's large civilian personnel. On shopping expeditions, in accordance with army regulations at the time, she was accompanied by her strapping husband, who was trained to walk into shops ahead of her and stand with his back against the back wall, revolver in hand, ready for possible terrorist attack.

His on-duty hours were spent scouring the mountain crags in a fruitless search for the hideout of Archbishop Makarios, leader of the guerilla fighters striving to bring about union with Greece.

Life, if you didn't happen to be a Cypriot, was exciting and full of fun. The young Angels revelled in it. Every free hour saw them basking on the beach where Aphrodite, goddess of love, had risen from the waves. Like a legendary hero, Tony plunged into the sea to rescue his bride when she floated too far out on her inflatable bed, too engrossed in watching marine life through a glass-bottomed biscuit tin to notice her danger.

At night, bronzed and god-like, his hair bleached blond by the sun, he rose to his feet to entertain the troops in a local nightclub. In a pleasant light baritone voice, he crooned 'Moonlight becomes you' and 'That's why the lady is a tramp,' in the style of his idol, Sinatra. He started to learn to play classical guitar and the saxophone, but was too much diverted by rally-driving to stick at the practice.

As the peak of the terror in Cyprus passed, they were able to leave the confines of the army base and rent part of a villa on a dirt road lined with stunted trees in the little port of Larnaca. For company they had a resident chameleon which earned its board by eating moths and flies, though it couldn't cope with the stick insects which often struggled into their bedroom at night through the gaps between the slats of the wooden shutters.

Monica increased her standing in the eyes of her Cypriot landlady by becoming pregnant and when she gave birth to a son, beautiful even by Greek standards, she achieved the status of a madonna. Tony got so staggeringly drunk on the night the child was born, he had to spend the next day searching for his white convertible, because he couldn't remember where he had parked it.

His and Monica's mothers travelled from England to see their grandson and found Tony to be an attentive, if occasionally misguided father. When the two grannies vied for who should cuddle the sleeping infant, he told them, 'You can play with him if you like, so long as he's quiet like this when you put him down.'

The smallest Angel continued to be the centre of his adoring family's attention when they returned to the UK at the end of the tour of duty in Cyprus.

Tony left the army to face the hazards of civilian life, where responsibility cannot be passed up the line or demeaning tasks delegated downwards. That same physical presence that made him an ideal soldier had the knack of arousing resentment in petty officials and an urge in them to take him down a peg.

Early on he drew attention to himself by being fined for driving the wrong way down a one-way street twice in one day, going in opposite directions. He had left home in the morning and driven into the street as had been his habit before he went away, not realising it had been made one-way and not noticing the signs until a warden stopped him. Returning in the afternoon, he turned into the street from the other end and was pulled up by the same warden who hadn't bothered to tell him the one-way system was to be reversed that day.

The family moved to a bungalow in a small Sussex town when their second son was born. It was almost reduced to three again when the new arrival was fed the wing nut from his carrycot by his two-year-old brother. Tony got a job selling mattresses. The going was hard at first, cold-calling on buyers who were only willing to see reps at certain times in the afternoon and then treated them with the British disdain for hawkers.

Things didn't improve until he took up golf. He set about learning the game with a single-minded determination, until he was proficient enough to challenge experienced players at the club. One of these proved to be chairman of a chain of furniture stores and within weeks, Tony's fortunes began to rise. Mattress sales increased sharply, and within months he was Area Sales Manager. Ironically, promotion marked the beginning of his downfall in the mattress-selling business. Salesmen under his management did not have the same access to purchasing power and the impetus could not be maintained. Lines on the sales graphs began to show a slow-down in the rate of climb and the job came to an end.

He got another as an executive with a building firm and he kept up his golf. His wife found herself often alone with her baby boys, while Tony got in practice at every possible moment. So addicted did he become, that when a fall of snow covered the course, he painted some balls red, in order to be able to continue practising. Eventually, his efforts were rewarded when he became the holder of the Farnham Frigate – a magnificent, silver-plated model galleon – trophy for the club's overall champion.

To his little sons, he was Superman and in his turn, he set

about making his firstborn in his own image. The child was exceptionally bright and flowered with the attention of his adoring parents. As a confident, well-mannered four-year-old, he could read, write and swim. The younger child had the charm but lacked not only his brother's stunning good looks and sharpness of intellect but like most second children did not enjoy the same degree of intense interest from his mother and father. He was destined to trail in his brother's shadow.

Tony was concerned to give his gifted boy the best possible start and arranged for him to be interviewed by the head of a private preparatory school with a reputation for academic excellence. He was accepted on the strength of his outstanding ability and his brother went too. The little family had all the trappings of success; father rising in his career, children in a good school and mother well groomed and competent. She was a good manager, dressing neatly on what she saved by prudent housekeeping. Tony provided well and liked to make the occasional magnificent gesture.

On her birthday one year, he presented her with a tiny gift-wrapped box containing a set of ignition keys, then led her to the window to see a shiny second-hand Mini parked at the kerb, tied in an outsize pink bow. But such extravagances had to be his idea; on holiday in Spain, when Monica fell in love with a suède suit and begged to have it, he refused and they had a bitter quarrel.

She was a woman of strong moral principles who, though not a churchgoer, was sustained by a quiet faith that Tony could not altogether share. He preferred not to dwell on the matter. Death was too remote to bother about, but his hedonistic enjoyment of life was marred by a fear that God might actually exist.

He blamed his wife's ambition to live in ever-improving style for the debts that began to accumulate. Discussion of the problem with her was not an option. To do so would be to diminish in her eyes. He simply had to increase their income to cover all the outgoings, which he did by simply taking a pound from each of the wage packets that he made up every week. It meant tweaking the PAYE figures only a tiny bit and if anyone noticed, the discrepancy was very slight. When the inevitable discovery came, Tony was faced with a choice between confessing to his wife before the CID arrived to question him or leaving realisation to hit her when the officers were on her doorstep.

According to his account, he got home ahead of the police and told her everything. She did not bravely offer to support and stand by him as he had hoped but reacted so angrily it sent him rushing to Beachy Head with the intention of flinging himself over the cliff. Possibly he set off on his suicide mission without ever going home, leaving Monica and her little boys to find that their lives were shattered when the police brought his letter of farewell.

It is not possible to know at what point on his desperate drive to the coast Tony changed his plan. Certainly by the time he reached Beachy Head he had decided a death leap was not the way for him. He may by then have seen the opportunity to start afresh or the idea may not have come to him until, as he claimed, he was striking out into the sea.

The first dramatic moves were carefully considered; after that, everything was left to chance. He wrote his suicide note then abandoned his car and made his way down to the beach. Leaving his outer clothing in a neat pile with the note weighted on top, he walked into the sea and headed for the horizon.

The water was cold and it was growing dark. After a while, he turned and swam along the coast, still going strongly and smoothly. Death was not going to come quickly and easily, he thought as he swam. Away on the shore, lights gleamed in a golf clubhouse. Familiar territory, a haven. He turned again and in a short time was standing on the shingle, almost as naked as the day he was born.

He crossed the links without being seen and skirted the clubhouse until he found the locker room. He got in easily and taking one of the towels he found laying about, had a shower. If anyone had come in, there would have been nothing to arouse suspicion, but he was not disturbed. He found clothes to fit and broke into lockers to find money, a cheque book and credit cards. John Allen now emerged; Anthony John Angel was washed away to sea.

John headed for the North. He had enough to see him through those first tightrope-walking days, but he needed to acquire substance quickly. The cheque book and credit cards were used freely to find him somewhere to stay temporarily and to buy clothes, a wallet, a suitcase and the thousand trivial possessions essential to life. He knew these were bridging strategies. He needed a job. But, without a P45, or employment records of any kind, he had no choice but to look in those areas where such details are often overlooked in the interests of filling jobs people might otherwise be unwilling to take.

His first job was on the night shift in a large bakery. His task was to inject the blob of jam into the centre of the doughnuts, though this story might have been concocted because it was an amusing yarn to spin to a bunch of blokes at a bar. From the bakery he progressed to a well-known firm making domestic appliances where he checked finished washing machines for faults. Every tenth one was clouted with a hammer to make enough dents to keep the boys in the repairs department in steady employment. It was hardly challenging work, but he opened a bank account and the identity of John Allen began to take concrete form.

Casual work in catering led on to better opportunities. He took advantage of training schemes offered by the Rank Organisation and rose rapidly from frying hamburgers in a fast-food café to become a skilled head waiter. The life suited him. He enjoyed being among people taking their leisure, ensuring their enjoyment. It was a branch of the show business he had always hankered after. Survival ceased to be his overriding preoccupation. While he was working in a Manchester night-club, he met Pat Walker and a love affair waiting to happen.

John needed a woman as he needed air to breathe. To him Pat embodied all those joys he had lost with the drowning of Tony Angel – love, warmth and a companion glamorous enough to make him the envy of other men. He set about winning her with dedicated enthusiasm.

2

John Allen – Bigamist, Bungler, Bankrupt

Few men, even those who actually like women, really know how to please one. John knew. He was valiant in his first passionate declaration of his feelings, not fearing rejection and when none came, he showed his appreciation of Pat by freely expressing his love and by a courtly attentiveness, anticipating and gratifying small wishes, laughing with her and being her loving companion.

As a lover he was ardent, considerate and skilful, though sometimes, after making love, he would be overcome by remorse in case he had offended. He wanted to own Pat, insanely trying to make her part of himself by buying her sweaters and jackets that matched his own, 'his and hers' shirts and, for them both, a pair of expensive sports watches, hers a smaller replica of his. She felt cherished – valued. Even brief partings were more than he could bear and within weeks of meeting her, he was begging her to live with him, but though she found his impetuosity endearing, she was too level-headed and down-to-earth to compromise over what she wanted.

Pat, a petite, blonde Yorkshire woman, had only just returned to England after living in Canada and the United States for ten years with an American Air Force officer. Before that, there had been marriage at twenty-one to one Marcus Walker which ended in separation after little more than a year. She was ready to settle, but wanted more than a live-in love affair. She was looking for commitment.

Always eager to give a lady what she craved, John arranged a special licence and they were married. Mr and Mrs John Allen set up home in Cheshire. He probably never told her about Monica and his boys. If he did, he would probably have explained that they were divorced but that he never had any contact with them because he felt it was best for the children. Pat may have believed this was his first marriage. He was happy in it, she knew that, the new man, taking a camera with him when he went with her to the delivery room, to record Jonathan's birth.

They were both thrilled to have Victoria just over a year later, but their fecundity was a little alarming and reproduction could not be allowed to go on at that rate. John agreed to have a vasectomy. In later years, when relations between him and Pat were strained, he used to drop his vasectomy into conversation when he was hoping to make a new conquest. In company that he knew very well, he would set a table laughing by boasting that the operation had to be done twice. Tests after the first snippings showed his indomitable sperm to be still present and he had to heroically face the whole procedure again.

Strain in their relationship was still unthinkable when, one day, walking down a street in Manchester, someone saw him and recognised the long-believed 'dead' Tony Angel and went to the police.

In court, he pleaded guilty to charges of bigamy, theft and obtaining money by false pretences. He asked for 116 other offences to be taken into consideration. Each stolen cheque and each use of a stolen credit card counted as an offence. He was given a suspended jail sentence of two years. Pat forgave him. She sat in court and afterwards took his hand as they walked out. He swore to make it up to her.

Bigamy is a senseless, pathetic crime. In his attempt to bend reality to make it fit his fantasy, John had delivered a terrible insult to both women. He either couldn't grasp the concept of 'an honourable estate', or he cared nothing for it. While he had been happily enjoying his illegal bliss, his true wife had been struggling to free herself from a grim situation. It had been difficult to explain to two bewildered little boys why their father had vanished. The house had had to go and she accepted her mother-in-law's offer to have her and the boys to live with her in the house on the Avenue.

Kitty was glad to have the children running about, it compensated her in part for the death of her son. Eventually, she took charge of the child care so that their mother could train for a new career. The two women became very close. They reacted differently, though, when newspaper reports of the court case in Manchester uncovered the fake suicide. Kitty's joy at finding he was still alive outweighed her anger. She forgave him; his wife couldn't. She could not bear to hear his name mentioned. Her bitterness deepened into an implacable hatred that in years to come was to alienate her from one of her sons.

Kitty found herself in the difficult situation of having to keep even telephone conversations with Tony a secret. She never did learn to call him John. They did not meet again until they both went to a family wedding. Kitty walked past him in church without recognising him. He was a burly eighteen stone.

'My God,' she said in disbelief, 'you look like an old man.'

It had already upset him when he'd had to pay over the odds for his new wedding suit. The tailor explained that he couldn't cut the jacket from one piece of cloth. His mother's failure to recognise him gave him the extra jolt he needed to go on a diet.

His doctor handed him a standard diet sheet. She was looking for a steady loss of three pounds a week. He was to go back in a fortnight. It was not good enough for John, he wanted instant restoration of his slim shape. He put himself on a regime of dry biscuits and water and at the end of two weeks, had lost a stone. Wearing the same clothes, he presented himself to be weighed, his pockets weighed by bags of coins to give a reading to please his doctor. In three months he lost six stones, but a weakness for sauté potatoes and ice cream was never mastered and wild fluctuations in his weight became a pattern.

Monica divorced him, and he was legally married, not in a discreet ceremony, but with a splash, Pat wearing an extravagantly flowered hat. They left the babies with an au pair and went off to honeymoon in a first-class hotel.

Some of his father's notions of discipline and insistence on politeness had rubbed off and he was strict with the kids, punishing them by hitting them on the hand with a ruler. Jonathan had it drummed into him that it was his duty to protect his little sister. They were expected to earn their pocket money. For their age, they were amazingly well mannered and self-possessed.

The family moved about a good deal, from Cheshire to Leicester to Northants, as John made his frequent job changes, usually to progress up the ladder. He spent a short time as Peter Sellers' valet. Fame and glamour attracted him. He loved it when an old manor where he was working as hotel manager was used to shoot some of the scenes in an historical film.

Pat had her hands full with the two children but once they had started at a small private school, John began to suggest ways she might find an interest outside the house and help to swell the family income. He always had his eye open for small business opportunities and his own efforts at dieting had alerted him to the money to be made from the national mania for slimming.

They borrowed the money to open a slimming salon and Pat was installed to run it. Diet sheets were handed out but the mainstays of the business were the machines which massaged and vibrated muscles to tone them and smooth away excess flesh. It may have been lack of enthusiasm on Pat's part, or the customers may have proved the machines didn't work by stubbornly remaining puddings, but the enterprise failed and the salon closed owing money.

He had an idea for a device called a 'Rac Mac', which aroused some interest among manufacturers. It was to be a waterproof cover to be incorporated into roof racks on cars which could be raised in wet weather to protect the baggage. He didn't follow it through and the idea came to nothing.

He kept his eyes and ears open for opportunities and, in the early seventies when the Post Office workers staged a protracted strike for more pay, he saw a chance to make money by providing private mail delivery. It covered Manchester only at first, but he was soon sending Pat as a courier to London with important packages and documents.

The service was efficient and reliable and beginning to expand when the strike ended and the Post Office reasserted its monopoly. He might have continued modestly as a courier but the idea lacked appeal and he decided against it.

There were two or three sacks of mail still awaiting delivery and he had to deal with those before he could consider the venture closed. A quick inspection revealed that they contained mainly circulars. Nothing to concern him. The swiftest, neatest solution he could think of was to burn them. He took the sacks to the corner of a public car park and lit a bonfire. He was seen and reported. Arrest followed on charges of interfering with Her Majesty's mail. The two years of his suspended sentence had not expired, but his defending counsel was confident he would get off with a fine or a further suspended sentence. He arrived in court sure that he would be going home that night.

The three years' custodial sentence left him in an almost catatonic state of shock. His only real recollection of his first day in Winson Green prison were of doors slamming and keys turning in locks.

He gave no trouble as a prisoner, hardly speaking, obeying the rules, always docile and obedient. Total withdrawal was his only survival strategy. Slopping out was loathsome to him and for the sun-worshipping John, confinement to a cell for twenty-three out of twenty-four hours was enough to bring him to breaking-point. He was becoming thin and gaunt when, towards the end of the first year, he was moved to an open prison. Life here was not unlike living in an army barracks. He resigned himself to counting the days to freedom. If he had to serve this sentence, then to do it here was bearable.

Pat was struggling with the kids in rented rooms. The house had been repossessed and John made bankrupt after the trial. She wrote and visited regularly, but he suspected that she had a lover. He realised that even her devotion might not withstand another such severe test. He need not have worried. When his release came after a year, his exemplary behaviour having earned him full remission of the residue of his sentence, she was waiting to take him home.

They tried to recapture that rapturous involvement with each other that they had known when they first met, but it did not happen again. If they had analysed their feelings they would have known it was impossible. No matter what he achieved in the future, he could never be to her the loving protector and benefactor of his fantasy. She had seen his frailty and thereby condemned their love to death.

Getting a job proved to be not too difficult. He hadn't lost the knack of impressing prospective employers and he invented the story of a prolonged stay in hospital to explain why he had been out of circulation. His fortune began to pick up again.

They got a house, possibly through Pat taking out the mortgage, since bankruptcy precluded him from holding a bank account, and achieved a kind of domestic harmony. They bought a basset-hound and named her Fleur after a character in a current TV serial. John was occasionally unfaithful, not with a particular lover, but whenever the opportunity presented – with a neighbour once, and occasionally with a lone hotel guest. Pat discovered one liaison and for several months they were estranged but he begged forgiveness and she decided to try again.

The New Grand Hotel in Torquay advertised for a banqueting manager and, being perfectly type-cast, John walked into the role. It meant another house move, but it was a step up and a fresh start in a new area.

Torquay didn't hold him long, though the town appealed to him and gave his family a period of stability and security. It had much in common with Bournemouth and he liked the night-life, the beaches and its good schools. He was doing well at the New Grand but, always on the lookout for something better, the restaurant manager's post in Salcombe's Marine Hotel enticed him away. He applied and with the help of excellent references from his employer, he landed the job.

Pat fell under Salcombe's spell. She loved the pretty waterfront and the smart little shops. The hotel allocated them a roomy maisonette in Powderham Villa, the staff house, and gave her a free hand to redecorate. The children had a bedroom each and the front windows looked out over rooftops to the harbour. She quickly made friends with the mothers of other young children when she took Vicky and Jonathan to school.

John's shifts were split to cover breakfast and lunch, a break in the afternoon, then back to supervise dinner in the evening. On Thursdays he stayed after work to play cards late into the night with three or four of the men on the staff.

Pat didn't mind. He seemed more content and she dared to hope they might settle at last. They were spending more time together as a family. John bought a seventeen-foot boat and after school, he took them all on fishing trips.

The tiny cabin had everything packed into it, two berths, a stove and, under one of the seat squabs, a chemical toilet which intrigued little Vicky. She made her parents laugh by sitting on the loo, loudly singing nursery rhymes as they skimmed over the waves.

John consulted local experts about the right fishing tackle and what sort of gear to wear so as not to look like a tourist. He got one of the fishermen to show him a good place to catch mackerel, but he never had much luck. It didn't matter, having a boat was the thing, one day he'd get a bigger, better one, go to navigation classes and cruise the Mediterranean.

He was an innocent in the great waters beyond the bar. He took one of the waiters out for the afternoon, taking a straight course out of the harbour to where he had been told there was a shingle bank below the surface, playground for shoals of fish. 'We'll tie up to that marker buoy ahead,' he told his companion.

They sped on and were almost within grappling distance of the buoy when it turned through ninety degrees and moved rapidly away. They had come within a whisker of trying to rope the fin of a basking shark.

Once a week he took Pat out to dinner. There were plenty of restaurants to choose from and he hadn't been to the Galley. He'd met Charlie Yabsley once when he came in to the Marine with a group of people for a drink and a post-mortem on a council meeting. He hadn't liked him much but he couldn't fail to be aware of the man's popularity and, when it came, the impact of his death. The funeral closed the shops and drained the town of people.

He hadn't met his widow but had heard a little about her. Everyone said she couldn't make a go of running the restaurant. It was known all over the county as 'Charlie's' and would never be the same without him.

Curiosity took him along on a wet dark night in mid-February. He found her sitting apart in the bar area, the tables at the far end of the long room surprisingly well filled with people in the last stages of dinner. She was wearing a long dress and doing the crossword. She got up to greet him when he came in.

He watched her as she moved among the diners, pouring coffee, fetching coats and his pity and interest were aroused.

He thought her quite beautiful, about forty years old, slim, dark haired, five feet four or so. Her voice pleased him, the conversation revealing that she was not as ignorant of the complexities of restaurant management as he had supposed; still, it was a lot for a woman with children to cope with alone.

The restaurant was well appointed. Heavy curtains blanked out the big window he had seen from the water. It was perhaps a bit too high and too long to make it easy to maintain a good atmosphere when it was only half full, but these clients were relaxed enough and a bit of attention to the lighting would work wonders.

She brought a tray of coffee and sat beside him at the end of the bar. When she got up to say good-bye to a departing customer, he picked up the paper and filled in several squares on the grid. She came back to peer over his shoulder, and he could feel her eyes on his face, studying him. They worked on at the crossword until the last diner left and the staff went home. He rose to go and she walked with him to the door, bidding him a polite good night. As the lock clicked behind him, he realised he had left his silver pen behind. He would have to go back.

3

Eunice's Story
– My Life Before Marriage

From all the jumbled images of places, faces and things that make up the memories of infancy, the first to come clearly into focus was the back yard behind the 'blocks'. A stony, grassless place, surrounded by high walls, with, if memory serves, a row of rabbit hutches along one side, and a chicken-run on the other. At the far end, almost against the wall, two air-raid shelters faced each other.

The 'blocks' were blocks of four flats standing in one of the better streets on the Isle of Dogs in London's East End, an island formed on three sides by the great horseshoe loop of the Thames and, on the fourth, by the West India Dock. A wooden staircase ran up from the pavement between the two lower flats to the landing between the front doors of the two above. A second stair descended to the communal yard. Two lavatories opened off it, serving the four families.

There was just enough room behind the shelters for me and my friend Joycie from across the yard to play in the dirt unseen from the house. A favourite game was to take a piece of stick and scrape the earth from a large stone in pretence of peeling potatoes. Joycie sometimes used to eat the dirt. My mother would remonstrate, and fought a one-sided battle for cleanliness. Scrubbing was her constant occupation. The hands that reached down to me were damp and smelled of Sunlight soap. When she pulled up my knickers in the morning, my head was pressed against a patch of flowery apron wet from the washing board. Despite all the scrubbing,

Joycie died of diphtheria. All the neighbours came out to watch the little white coffin being carried out. I stood outside our front door at the foot of the stairs and watched the procession. The man upstairs, who drove a van and wore a livery, followed Joycie's father. As he passed, I saw myself reflected in his polished green gaiters.

We shared our shelter with the family of the man with the gaiters. The shelter had a couple of bunks, a kitchen chair used as a step down from outside, and a hand-pumped respirator for my baby brother in case of a gas attack. When he grew bigger he was given a Mickey Mouse gas mask which I coveted. The shelter was always half-full of water and had to be continually baled out. My mother planted sunflowers on top for camouflage and, by September 1940, they had grown tall enough to tangle with the washing line.

The baby's arrival on a bitter day in the winter before had been the most significant event of the year. The only heating had been the fire in my mother's bedroom, from which my big sister Connie and I were barred. We huddled round the gas stove as my father, still wearing a balaclava, cooked food for us. When I was allowed to see my mother and was shown the reason for my misery, a white bundle with a pink ball in the middle, I was not greatly impressed.

I knew there was 'Hitler', and 'Germans', which were somehow menacing, because my parents kept saying they were nothing to worry about. I did not let them disturb my play, though peeling potatoes was no fun without Joycie, nor was having to sit without moving or speaking while my father listened to the news on the wireless. Early one sunny evening, the air-raid warning sounded and Connie beat me across the yard to be first to drag away the huge piece of T-iron holding the shelter door closed. We were closely followed by people from the other flats, jostling, exclaiming and pointing upwards. High above, the sky behind the sunflowers was darkening with approaching aircraft. The growling noise which had begun as the siren slurred away, strengthened and swelled until the ground vibrated. As we watched, other planes rose and advanced to meet them. Fire began streaking back and forth and black-winged shapes would buck and twist, then spiral down, buzzing like stricken bluebottles. The air became loud with gunfire, explosions and the whistle of falling bombs.

When the first hot shrapnel pinged against the building, we were bundled into the shelter. The adults stayed above to watch the battle. From below we could hear their incredulous shouts. 'The rum quay's bought it', cried one, and, another, 'The Albert Dock's getting a pasting.' A bomb found its target in the street outside and the adults joined us underground. The all-clear at dawn coaxed us up, dirty and sleepless, to take stock of our changed surroundings. We stood huddled together in the dust-laden air. No one shouted. Our block was still standing, but one of the women pointed to a great crack running from ground to roof. The windows were gone. So, too, was my little back-yard world.

My parents decided that night to take us off the island, fearing that we would be trapped if one of the bridges were hit. We set out to walk north for a mile or so, to where bridges spanning dock entrances from the river linked the island to Limehouse and the rest of the East End. My mother pushed the baby in the pram, a small zinc bath balanced on top, containing food and what she considered essentials. Connie walked beside her, holding on to the handle. I rode on my father's shoulders, my fingers entwined in his crisp black hair. The way off the island lay along the perimeter road, a cobbled treeless track, with high dock walls on either side. Elevated as I was, they towered, grim and black, above me. Flames leapt above the wall and I could see cranes, like pokers drawn from the fire, glowing red against the inky sky. Smoke and burnt paper blew against my face.

We drew near a bridge, passing exhausted firemen, sitting heads in hands on the kerb. Hoses trailed across the road to a thin trickle of river. The tide was out; the mains were hit and there was no water to fight the acres of fire. Sightseers had crowded on to the bridge, impeding the passage of the pram into Poplar. It was hardly sanctuary, but from there further flight was possible.

That night we slept in the basement passage of a house in Oriental Street, where relatives lived, crowded in with many other people. Other nights were spent in public shelters, where I was thrilled to be given a bunk with rough white sheets, and on underground station platforms, where we found what comfort we could. There was a brief period of stability when we occupied part of a house in Catford. Empty houses were not difficult to come by in London at that time.

My mother went back to the island at least twice, leaving us with an aunt. In the urgency to leave the island, she had forgotten that our corner grocer had cut our ration coupons out of the books, a forbidden practice; he was supposed to cross them off in indelible pencil. Without them, we couldn't eat. She caught a bus to the subway running between Greenwich and the island, but found the tunnel was full of water, and a ferryman was rowing people across the Thames. The street, when she reached it, was roped off. And unexploded landmine, parachute still attached, had caused a crater in the road. An ARP (air-raid precautions) workman had laid a plank across the hole which lay between her and the grocery shop. She explained her mission. He eyed her ample frame: 'I can't carry you across.'

'Who the bleeding hell asked you to? I can do the same as you, walk across!'

She walked the plank, looking down on what she described as 'A bleeding big thing, all polished precision, sent to blow us sky-high.'

Inside the shop, Mr Rowell the grocer was packing things from the shelves into boxes, apparently unconcerned about what lurked outside his door. He couldn't provide the coupons, she would have to brave bureaucracy and apply for duplicates, but: 'Here,' he said, 'take some of this stuff with you.' They filled a box with as much as she could carry and she tottered back across the plank.

On her way home she called at the Food Office in Poplar library, to get replacement ration books. Officials tried to send her to another branch, but her temper, never on a long fuse and formidable to behold, snapped.

'I have got three hungry little kids waiting for me in Catford. So get your bleedin' fingers out. I haven't got a thing to eat in the house!'

Telling us this later, she grew breathless with laughter: 'I'd got it all with me, in a box!' She got her coupons and made the tortuous journey back, stressed because she had laddered her stockings getting back into the rowing boat.

The bombing kept us moving from place to place for the next two years. Father was frequently absent for long periods. We didn't know it at the time, but he was engaged in welding PLUTO, the pipeline under the ocean. Somehow he and my mother contrived to appear unafraid, so that though we had moments of fear, we were confident of our survival. Connie even managed to pass a scholarship to a grammar school, despite having snatched her primary education in a succession of schools and front rooms. News of her success came in the post just after yet another change of address. We had been in residence in a house in Barking for no more than a couple of days when the letter arrived. Mother was beside herself with joy. She ran out to the front gate to tell someone but, knowing no one in the area, came back indoors to dance up and down in the kitchen. Still excited, she delivered me for my first day at the new infants' school round the corner. It was long and low with a verandah in front. I spent playtime standing, marvelling, under a lilac in bloom in the play-ground. At half-past three, I stood near the gate waiting for her to collect me, but she didn't come. She had forgotten me. The last of the other mothers left and I was alone, not knowing which way to go, so I dealt with the situation in characteristic fashion. I opened my mouth and bawled.

A policeman materialised and tried to read the address on my battered gas-mask case, but it was unreadable or had not been updated. I told him my name and what detail I could remember about the house, which was that it had a bay window, a feature that had particularly pleased my mother. He took my hand and we were walking along together, presumably towards the police station, when I recognised the green frilly curtains and knew I was found.

One of the creeds by which my mother lived was always to have clean windows and fresh curtains. Others were: feed and defend the family; never get into debt; and abide by the teachings of her Catholic upbringing. Distilled into their essence, these seemed to be: despise non-Catholics, and sex outside marriage is the unforgivable sin. She was none too certain about sex within marriage either. It was still the era of the stork and the gooseberry bush.

Hers was a mixed marriage. She and Father had known each other since he used to shout rude names at her as they passed, she on her way to the Catholic school, he going to the one run by the Church of England. He refused to bring up their prospective children as Catholics, so she could not marry in a Catholic church. They rectified this thirty years later by going through a second ceremony.

Religion was a sore point between them, so they agreed not to mention it. The subject was taboo in the household, which was probably the reason for my getting religion rather badly when I was eight years old. I kept my mouth shut about it but it affected my behaviour. I gained a reputation for obedience and docility. Connie thought me a prig. I caught the condition from the terrifying headmistress of my junior school. It was co-ed, a situation forced on the local Education Committee by the RAF having taken over the boys' building and the scarcity of teachers. Every able-bodied person was fighting or doing war work.

We were taught in classes of forty-five or fifty. The three Rs, scripture and gas-mask drill. I desperately wanted to go to grammar school but had a dreadful, lurking fear that I was not as clever as Connie. I based this on the fact that Mother had told me so and that I could not get any of my sums right, though I could remember a time, two or three schools ago, when I got them all right. The time for the scholarship exam came and Mother kept telling me not to worry, just do the best I could and it wouldn't matter if I didn't pass. I didn't pass and it did matter, a great deal, to me.

I passed a second, lesser scholarship, to a 'Secondary Modern' school, children being divided into three categories in those days, but the sense of failure and inferiority never left me. I became more withdrawn and bookish, saved only by my love of English from sliding to the very bottom of the academic ladder. The school was for girls only, existing to provide secretarial fodder for London commerce. I learned to phrase a business letter, but got thrown out of shorthand class for laughing uncontrollably. I had been reading *Three Men in a Boat* under my desk. I was not a great success at domestic science either, largely because it was against my mother's principles to pay ninepence a week for the ingredients of the rock cakes. She objected to any hint of compulsion, but this could not be explained to an irate school teacher.

At fifteen, the school arranged job interviews for us, and on New Year's Day 1950 I began work as a half-hearted library assistant at St Bride's Institute, just off Fleet Street. Arranging books on shelves in alphabetical order was tedious even for a book lover. I did not shine in this or in the job as filing clerk which followed. There was one bright interlude at stage-struck sixteen, when in response to an impassioned letter written to the manager of one of London's theatres, I was allowed to go and work as an assistant stage-manager. It involved making coffee, ironing costumes and running errands. Had I stuck it out I might one day have been given a walk-on part, but there was no pay and the tube fare was half-a-crown a day. It was impossible.

A pity, really. I might have excelled in well-rehearsed situations. Everyday encounters found me tongue-tied and in an agony of embarrassment, particularly if a boy showed interest. While my peers were finding release from their similarly mind-numbing jobs in dance halls, at the pictures and in the general thrill of hunting for a mate, my pleasures were taken solemnly and usually alone. Snob that I was, I wanted to escape from the way of life of a whole social class.

There seemed only one route open to me. At eighteen I was accepted for nurse training at the London Hospital, Whitechapel. I might have seized the chance to get out of London and applied to train somewhere in the country, but the London was esteemed by East Enders and I had grown up thinking of it as 'the hospital'. It did not occur to me to apply anywhere else.

Obedience and docility were useful attributes for the student nurse in the 1950s. Entering hospital was still akin to entering a convent. Matron ruled, running the huge empire that was the London with the combined skills of a Mother Superior, a Chancellor of the Exchequer and an Admiral of the Fleet. At my interview, which was long and with her alone, she spoke much about vocation, selflessness and devotion to duty. I was given the opportunity to explain my motives, though the word was never used, for wishing to be a nurse. I remember saying I wished 'to justify my existence'. She seemed to find this a perfectly reasonable sentiment for an eighteen-year-old.

There was no waiting for a decision. She referred to no committees or panels. She made up her mind to take me, and before I left the hospital I was given my starting date and taken to the dressmaking department to be measured for my uniforms. There were six months to wait until the first intake of students after my eighteenth birthday. I spent them paying off weekly instalments on a watch with a sweep second hand, from Mother's mail-order catalogue. The regulation brown lace-up shoes with the orthopaedically correct two-inch heel were to be fitted once we entered preliminary training school.

This was an elegant old mansion close to Bow Bridge in the East End, with a huge walled garden. There we spent six weeks learning anatomy and physiology, bandaging, bedmaking, a smattering of invalid cookery and other basic nursing skills. From the first we were addressed as 'nurse'. Before breakfast at eight we were supervised in an hour's housework. With so many hands and such hawk-eyed supervision, the house gleamed in every cranny. In the hall was a large notice, on which was written 'Speed with Efficiency'.

Towards the end of the six weeks we spent an evening helping in a ward. It was a tremendous shock, despite the careful preparation. The sights and smells were sickening enough, but the sound of rattling coughs made me retch. On my first evening I was asked by another student to help change the bed of a patient who had been incontinent of faeces. I gritted my teeth and accomplished the task without my colleague realising how close I was to vomiting. My set were fortunate in that metal sputum pots had recently been replaced by waxed, lidded pots, doing away with the revolting job of scrubbing them out after measuring the contents. If I had had to do that, I doubt if I would have stayed the course.

One week working full-time in my first ward cured me of my squeamishness, though it was six months before I adjusted to the new life. Within a year I had been jerked by the scruff of the neck from idealistic teenager into something approaching maturity.

Night duty in the second year was as testing a time as it was designed to be. In each year of training, three months were spent on night duty, a first-year student continuing in her role as general dogsbody, attached to one ward, with a staff nurse as her mentor. In the third year, as a senior student, she would take charge of half of one of the wards which were divided into two sections of fourteen beds. In staff nurse's absence she had overall charge. Second-year students were used as relief staff, filling any of these roles as required.

Night duty meant sometimes arriving in a strange ward at 8.30, completing the evening routine and settling patients to sleep by about 10.30, leaving half an hour or an hour at most to memorise the Kardex. This was a card-index system for storing information about each patient, arranged in order of bed number. Night sister did three rounds of each ward every night. On the first, which could take place any time between 11pm and 1am, it was required that she be escorted from bed to bed by the nurse in charge. They would stand together by the bed, sister with torch in hand to light the charts hanging at the foot, and nurse would give the patient's name, diagnosis and details of treatment given during the day. Having learnt the facts in the order in which they appeared in the Kardex, it was disconcerting if sister, feeling bloody-minded, decided to start with the last bed first, or zig-zagged her way round. It was a tremendous feat of memory. We lived in dread of night sister, who, in her two-year spell of night duty, developed the eyesight of a black cat stalking its prey.

Not all her questions were relevant to patients. Some were meant to catch you out and keep you properly terrorised. A favourite was to ask a nurse new to the ward, the name of the sub-division, or second side. I was lucky that when I had glanced at the embossed board above the fireplace, the title had imprinted itself on my mind, so when the broadside was fired, I was able to reply 'Gore, sister'.

Most of my second spell of night duty was spent in a male medical ward. It coincided with one of the Great Fogs for which London was renowned. The ward rapidly filled with heavily dependent men with severe breathing difficulties. At one point, seventeen of the twenty-six patients were unable to get out of bed, wash or drink unaided. The whole hospital was under pressure so there was no hope of extra help. Washing and turning patients had to begin at four if bed-making and drug administration was to be completed before the day staff came on duty at 7.30.

At some time in the night, the report had to be written.

This had to be done with the same care as illuminating a mediaeval manuscript, beginning with the name and progress of the most seriously ill person, and descending until it concluded with a phrase such as 'the remaining patients slept well'. This had to be neatly written with pertinent observations underlined. After one night on which three old men died, their beds rapidly refilled with other distressed occupants, I failed to complete my report correctly. Soon after going off duty I was called to Matron's office. As I sat with other offenders on the row of upright chairs outside the door, I feel asleep, and slid to the floor. When shown the report by one of the assistant matrons, I saw that in one place, my writing had trailed off the line, the sentence left unfinished. No penalty was imposed. It's possible that it was recognised as an effect of sleep deprivation. If such sympathy was felt, it was not expressed.

Other quaint customs had grown up as in any ancient institution. Any communication with our superiors had to be submitted in writing; requests for days off and so on, ending with 'Please Sister'. This to be written on a slip of paper three inches by four, the corners then to be clipped off. Only octagonal requests were considered. Before returning from annual leave, we were required to write to Matron, saying how much we looked forward to going back.

In my third year, when I had just finished a long spell of night duty and was looking forward to four nights off, my parents suggested I go with them to Salcombe. They had been once before, with a neighbour who had been there as an evacuee. My brother Tony, by now a muscular eighteen-year-old, was going too. The plan was to travel overnight – the journey from London taking about nine hours before the motorway was cut – and to find a camp site when we arrived. By 7.30 in the morning, we were nearing Salcombe and Tony, searching in the campers' guidebook, said, 'There's a camp site on Beadon Farm, just on the outskirts of the town, run by a Mrs Yabsley.'

'What an ugly name,' I said.

We found the farm, and were turning down the rough track when a battered Austin Seven, its radiator bedecked with badges, the largest of which bore the legend 'Double Diamond Works Wonders', came hurtling towards us, appearing to leap lightly from hump to hump. The driver leaned out, smiling broadly and gestured to the field on his left, already blossoming with tents, and yelled, 'Just pull in anywhere.'

Looking wearily through the back window, I thought what sunny faces these sons of Devon have. Nothing more was said, but as he rocketed past, I saw that he was in naval uniform and that my presence had been noted.

We pitched our tent, a sort of igloo held upright by four inflatable tubes, and rested from our journey. From our position near the top of the long ridge, the land dropped steeply away. We could not see the valley floor. Wood-crowned hills on the far side swooped down to meet it. I could not name the things growing, but among the many shades of green, far below the old grey farmhouse was what I thought must be a field of corn. I sat with my back against a hedge, mesmerised as the wind rippled and shadowed its surface in mimicry of the sea.

Around 2pm, the Austin Seven reappeared in the lane, bumped the gate open with its nose and came haring up the steep incline to our camp. The driver got out, took a large chunk of rock from the car and wedged it behind the front wheel. He shook hands with my parents as though they were old friends long parted, then sprawled on the grass at my mother's feet.

Cockney hospitality demanded that tea be made and I occupied myself with the task unperturbed. He did not look like a suitor. Very short, he was no more than five-feet-three, stocky and in his mid-thirties.

4

Charles – Courtship and Marriage

Within a week of our meeting, Charles had asked me to marry him, an impetuous act for a man of thirty-six, but it was this recklessness, so different from my father's extreme caution, that attracted me.

He had endeared himself to my mother by moving us into a caravan when one of the inflatable struts on our tent got a puncture, leaving us enveloped in wet canvas in the middle of the night.

Once she knew that marriage was in prospect, she did what would otherwise have been unthinkable and agreed to go back to London without me. I could enjoy a few days of unofficial leave in which I could make up my mind. She had always held the opinion that any man would have to be 'bleedin' unusual' to interest me and Charles was certainly that.

His duties as sailing instructor at the Royal Naval College in Dartmouth didn't seem to detain him long. By lunchtime he was back and we would tear round Salcombe and the South Hams in the afternoons, seeing the places and people he loved. Many of these proved to be pubs and publicans, but everyone greeted him with unfeigned pleasure.

He drove everywhere with his foot hard down, even on rough dirt tracks, putting into practice his theory that the ride was smoother if the wheels didn't have time to roll into the troughs.

I was alarmed the first time the Austin mounted the narrow pavement as we drove down Salcombe Fore Street, forcing a man to leap back into a shop doorway. I soon got used to it. It was just his affectionate recognition of a friend. I began to notice people pressing themselves against walls and hedges as they saw the little car coming; its progress often followed by cries of 'Charlie! You bugger ...'

There was no formal introduction to his family, he simply walked in with me, through the back door into the huge farm kitchen where a crowd seemed to be assembled. The din was unbelievable. Everyone was talking. An elderly, white-haired woman I took to be his mother, was sitting at the head of the vast table, crying and complaining loudly. A small, quite beautiful woman with dark hair was preparing a meal, her eyes screwed up against the smoke curling up from the cigarette clenched between her teeth.

A cloth had been laid in readiness for the meal at one end of the table; at the other, a third woman was polishing brass and copper. She remained quiet. The two men in the room were bellowing at each other, occasionally throwing remarks at the woman doing the cooking. No one appeared to be put out by my arrival, or to be concerned by their mother's distress until Alison, the cook, said in a throaty voice, 'Aw shut up Mother, have a fag.'

'Francis,' Charles bawled, 'this is Eunice. What do you think of her?'

The older of the two men looked at me and grinned: 'Her's 'andsome.'

'Francis is deaf,' Charles said, partially explaining why they were all yelling, then abandoned me and went to peer into the saucepans on the stove.

Alison took charge, treating me with an easy familiarity as if I had been walking in on their monumental family rows for years. She set a place for me next to her mother, who amazed me by confiding to a total stranger, the reasons for her misery.

I gathered that John (the younger man) was home from America on a visit with Nancy his fiancée. Nancy had stormed out of the house that morning and taken a flight home. I couldn't quite work out why, though Alison repeatedly interrupted her mother to offer bits of information, like: 'She even took out his shoe laces and scrubbed them.' In the midst of my bewilderment, I was impressed by this. It didn't fit in with my image of the liberated American woman at all.

The woman cleaning brass finished the task and got up to go, refusing pleas that she stay to lunch, saying that she had to get to the top of the lane in time to catch the bus.

'Good-bye, May,' they chorused.

'May is Richard's wife,' Alison explained. 'We always say, Dick plants his rhubarb in May.' At which she laughed raucously.

May had fended off a lunge from John and reached the back door, from where she gave me what I thought was a sympathetic smile. When she had gone, the mother started crying again. 'That dear maid,' she said, 'comes every Wednesday to help Alison turn out the bedrooms.'

'Mother is very feeling-hearted,' said Alison, who had been placing dishes on the table – roast beef, boiled rice, three or four vegetables, cream, junket, stewed fruit – until there was little of the cloth to be seen. I was surprised when Francis too took his leave. All this food was meant for the four of them, Mother, Alison, John and Charles. There was obviously no problem in providing for an unexpected visitor.

I learned that there were three more of them. Joan, Mary and Richard. Father had died the year before. Mary also lived in America, but came home fairly frequently. I met them eventually but never did see them all in the same room at one time.

Charles had leased Hangar Mill from his mother and had been working all that summer installing electricity and redecorating. He had intended to move out of the farmhouse and live an ideal batchelor existence there. Alison would clean and do the washing and he could continue to womanise free from his mother's scrutiny. Celibacy had no part in his scheme. He assured me there were always plenty of women around, thankful to receive his attention.

This paradise had had to be shelved for the moment. He was due to go to South Africa in the following January on a 'showing the flag' cruise with the Navy, so he had installed a Miss Thrupp as tenant. He took me to call on her.

Someone had thoughtlessly latched the field gate when we arrived, causing Charles to swear when it refused to yield to nudging from the Austin. I got out and opened it. The car passed through, but he wouldn't wait for me to close it or to get back in.

'Jump on the running board,' he shouted, and accelerated down the steep path at a teeth-rattling pace, with me clinging to the side. It was the first of many times that I covered the last bit of the journey home in such a fashion.

Hangar Mill was a smallholding belonging to Beadon Farm. Up until the 1920s local farmers had taken their grain there to be ground. Deep ruts from the wheels of farm carts had been worn into the granite outcrops that jutted through the surface of the narrow tracks converging on the complex of stone buildings.

It had once been a centre of rural industry. Iron ore had been washed there and, a few yards higher up the valley, was a disused pumping station which had provided the town with water, until the Avon was dammed.

Now, the pumping station stood behind a wire fence erected by the council and the great water-wheel of the mill was permanently stilled.

One of Charles' uncles had wrecked it by throwing it into gear at the wrong moment, tearing out some of the wooden cogs. The stream which fed the overshoot had been diverted higher up the valley and now gurgled along in front of the house, bypassing the mill leat. Much of the machinery remained, exposed to the sky, the roof having long since fallen in.

The range of barns and outbuildings lacked floors in some places and the row of pig styes was uninhabitable, even for pigs. Everything was in a state of picturesque dereliction, except for the cottage butting on to the mill, which was in good repair and had been freshly painted white.

The buildings were grouped together in a rough quadrangle at the head of a narrow valley running up from a sandy cove. Lush woods and fields swept down the hillsides to encircle them. To my slum-sore eyes, it seemed to have been lifted from a Kate Greenaway illustration in a book of fairy tales.

Charles chose me for his wife as his father had taught him to choose horses; with an eye open for a good all-purpose beast. Strong enough to pull the plough, yet smart enough to do him credit on the hunting field. Kind, bright eyes and a gentle demeanour. At least, that's what he claimed, though I came to understand, when I used to ponder on what it was about me that made him despise me so much, that in fact he had fallen deeply in love. He felt helpless and out of control, resenting me for the power it gave me over him.

If he had taken his analogy of the horse a little farther, he might have realised that, like that animal, I was unaware of my power and wouldn't know how to begin to misuse it.

The difference in our ages made us an unlikely couple and courtship between a sailor and a nurse is next to impossible. Once I had agreed to marry him, after my finals in November, he applied for and got a drafting to Chatham. I was doing my training in theatres at the London Hospital annexe in Brentwood, Essex, so the distance was reasonably commutable. It took him only two or three hours to drive, though since I didn't get off duty until 8.30pm and had to be back by 11, it often seemed to me to be hardly worth the effort. I tried to persuade him not to come every night, but he insisted.

One evening, just as I was coming off duty, a young boy was brought to the hospital with severe head injuries and I was summoned back to the theatre. There was just time to leave a note for Charles.

When I got out at 10.45, there was a message from him in Home Sister's office. He was waiting for me.

'He kept coming and rapping on the window,' the sister on duty told me. 'He could hardly see over the window sill, but he gave me such a lovely smile.' Clearly, she was charmed.

He wasn't smiling when I found him. He had passed the time at the pictures, watching a film about a circus act, in which Gina Lollabrigida ensnared Burt Lancaster with her beauty and held him captive to her will. He spent the few minutes we had together before my curfew complaining bitterly that I had ruined his life.

We could not be married in church because Charles was divorced. It had been a war-time marriage which lasted for only a few days. He had been sent overseas and didn't return for more than two years. When he came back, she had found someone else. They were both nineteen.

We had planned to marry without fuss on 18 December, in Kingsbridge Registry Office, but our plans changed when his mother threw me out of the house. I had been spending the few days before my wedding at Beadon and one night, she caught us creeping into the house after midnight. I had no option but to leave and, to her astonishment, Charles left with me. So, it was back to the caravan, this time in sinful cohabitation, a situation which had to be brought to a swift end, if only because it would outrage and upset my mother. I phoned her and told her the wedding had been brought forward to 12 December.

On that wet Wednesday morning, Francis reported that their mother had had a 'heart attack' and was leaving to stay with Joan in Colchester. Since it was plain that she could not

possibly do both, we decided to go ahead with the wedding.
I began to see why Nancy had departed so suddenly.

I had asked my family not to make the journey for what
would, for my mother, be a disappointing ten-minute
ceremony. When it was over, we crossed the road to the
King's Arms for a celebratory drink with Charles' best man and
life-long friend, Bill Yeoman. None of Charles' family came
either.

The honeymoon was to be a long week-end in London.
True, I had just come from there and had lived there all my
life, but Charles' father, Jimmy, had always taken Mabel, his
mother, to stay at the Piccadilly Hotel when the Smithfield
show was on in town and it followed that London was where
we would go too, though to stay at the Regent Palace, not
the Piccadilly.

It took at least eight hours in those days to cover the 250
miles from Salcombe to London, and we ran into freezing
fog. I hadn't learnt to drive and couldn't take a turn at the
wheel. It was very cold, the Austin had somehow lost a rear
window and I was about to get my first glimpse of his vitrio-
lic temper.

A signpost loomed out of the fog. 'What does it say?' he
demanded. I didn't answer immediately, a fatal mistake and,
had I had the benefit of naval training, one I would have
known not to make. You don't keep a Chief Petty Officer
waiting. I peered at the arm of the post, but could make
nothing out.

'What's the matter with your fucking eyes?' he snarled. His
bride of less than twenty-four hours was too shocked to answer.

He sailed for a year's cruise to South Africa on HMS
Mounts Bay at the end of January. He had tried to arrange an
accompanied trip, but the Royal Navy needed much longer
notice. He was generous and caring in many ways, providing
well for me by making me a weekly allowance from his pay.

The London offered me a post as staff nurse, but after

three and a half years in nurses' homes, I had a yen for some home life. My parents had moved with Tony to a bright modern house in Basildon New Town. I thought it would be nice to spend the year with them before going to live in Devon. I got a job as staff nurse in the eye unit at Southend General Hospital.

There were two small wards, one each for men and women, a few private rooms and a theatre. It was satisfying work. In sister's absence, I assisted in theatre, then nursed the patients post-operatively. Most of the adults were having lens extractions to correct cataracts, but I specially loved the toddlers who came in to have their squints straightened.

I used some of my new affluence to pay for driving lessons and when I passed my test, I looked around for a small car. I couldn't afford much, and a friend of my father's told me about an ancient MG, on the market for £45. I'd had a tax rebate and could just about scrape the money together.

I loved that car. It was a bright yellow 1931 Midget...built four years before I was born. It had been much modified, with its original 'duck tail' removed and a false slab tank added to give it a more up-to-date look. The wheels had wire spokes and, something which made men marvel, cable brakes and an overhead camshaft.

Brass anchor buttons held the bonnet flaps in place and a 1930s bathing belle adorned the radiator cap, her swim suit reaching down to her knees. The canvas hood was a little shabby.

It was a capricious little beast, running sweetly as a sewing machine, especially if the weather was damp, then drying up on me without warning or leaving me with no lights when I failed to notice that the dynamo wasn't charging. I became adept with a starting handle and at double-declutching.

I spent my half-days off polishing and cleaning it like a mantelpiece ornament. Even the engine, which was largely made of brass, gleamed. As soon as I could afford it, I sent it off to have a new hood fitted and new red upholstery.

Charles and I exchanged letters regularly. He was interested to hear about the MG and, when the time drew near for him to return, it was agreed that I should take it with me to Salcombe.

5

A Chief Petty Officer's Wife

Snow covered the West Country on the day of Charles' homecoming. It was the general opinion that the single-track section of the Plymouth road, which ran down the long steep hill into Aveton Gifford, would be perilous, so I abandoned my dream of motoring to the docks in the MG with the hood down and instead went in the taxi from Cranch's Garage to meet my husband.

As we crossed Laira Bridge into Plymouth, HMS *Opossum* was sailing up-channel with her paying-off pennant streaming behind her in the wind, proving the estimate of her time of arrival to be precisely correct. For a moment ship and taxi were neck and neck, then our courses diverged and I passed through the dock gates to join the other wives shivering on the quayside.

I could see him, as they came alongside, standing among the men pressed against the rail, waving with both arms above his head. Minutes later, he was swaying down the gangplank, a huge baggage roll over his shoulder.

On the journey home, he hugged and kissed me with the joyous enthusiasm of a wet labrador puppy. At one point, when I was allowed to come up for air, he picked up his cap and said, 'I got this for you in Capetown.' He probed behind the badge and brought out a diamond solitaire. 'I picked out the diamond myself, and had the ring made,' he said. It was the most valuable and beautiful thing I had ever been given.

I was thrilled to have it and glad I hadn't known its hiding place when we had passed the customs post.

There were more presents to come. Later that day, when we had seen his family and were alone at Hangar, we opened the baggage roll and laid the contents on the rug in front of the fire. He had bought something for me or for our home in every place the ship had called to show the flag. There were carved ebony figures from the west coast of Africa, inlaid brass plates, earrings, necklaces, a crocodile-skin handbag with a silver filigree bracelet inside and a silver cruet from Gibraltar. There was no parrot, but it was otherwise a perfect sailor's return.

The winter night closed in on North Sands Valley and we drew the sofa up to the fire. 'You won't regret marrying me,' Charles said. I looked around the tiny living-room, at the fire-light playing on the black beams and on the grandfather clock, and said, 'If we're not happy here, it will probably be our own fault.' It was to be the only evening of our entire marriage that we spent alone together by the fireside.

Beadon Farm, of which Hangar Mill was part, had once stretched to the sandy cove at North Sands. In the summer, Jimmy Yabsley used to open the valley fields behind the beach for campers. Charles loved to set the public bar in the Fortescue laughing with the story of how his father rigged up a rough screen from hessian nailed to four poles, installed a bucket and had struggled for days to persuade a door with a penny-in-the-slot mechanism to hang on the structure.

Leaving the farming to Francis, his firstborn, the old man would spend the sunny days sitting on the sea-wall watching the antics of the visitors. He kept a few ponies tethered nearby and would make a little money hiring them out for rides round the beach, gladly assisting any inexperienced young woman in a bathing suit to mount.

Like all coastal farmers in the West Country, when the boom in tourism began, he found himself under irresistible pressure to let people pitch tents and park caravans on his land.

The local council, anxious to bring the situation under control and with an envious eye on the potential revenue, served a compulsory purchase order, the price based on a valuation of the agricultural land arrived at by the district valuer. It was a fraction of its actual market value. The family resisted, but it was shown that the public good was at issue and it proved a one-sided fight. All that land adjoining the beach, extending for about 100 yards up the valley, fell into council ownership for the purpose of providing 'public walks and pleasures'. They promptly covered it with concrete and turned it into a fee-charging car park.

When I went to live at Hangar, the camp site was confined to the three or four fields at the top edge of the farm, where the farm was skirted by the main road. It was a modest operation, bringing in enough money to keep Mabel comfortable and to keep the house and land in good order. Probate had not yet been granted on James Yabsley's will, but it was known that he had left his estate, in various proportions, to his family.

Charles was a generous provider and enjoyed bringing me unlooked-for gifts. One of his friends who had a dress shop in the town often waylaid him as he drove through Fore Street, calling out from the doorway, 'Charlie, I've got just the thing for Eunice.' He would arrive at Hangar clutching a huge box, pause to pee on the clematis, then come in with his offering.

We went out a good deal. In the first months after his return we were seen in every hotel and restaurant in the area, and there were many. Sometimes, I went with him to Plymouth to go shopping while he was in the dockyard. Charles liked to arrive at any destination in the last second of the last minute before his due time, so the journey down was a thrilling sequence of bend-cutting and cornering on two wheels. Coming home was more leisurely; we stopped at every pub along the route. Not that his thirst was unquench-able, though his capacity for Double Diamond was remark-able; he just liked to chat to the landlords and check on who was drinking in the bars. The Fortescue and the King's Arms in Salcombe were the last two ports of call. There are three more pubs between them and Hangar, but these he would visit in rotation and not as a matter of daily routine.

One of Charles' first acts when he returned to duty after his leave had been to buy a roll of red lino for the kitchen floor. It was raining, so he made a hole in the hood of the MG and brought it home from Plymouth sticking through the roof. Soon after that he decided the MG was too unreli-able, and bought a Land Rover with a diesel engine. He had a tow bar attached, so that it could be used on the caravan site.

My car was pushed into the top barn at Hangar, where it stayed because, having no income of my own, I couldn't tax or insure it. I missed it, but since there was nothing that could be done, I got along without it and anyway, I was much taken with a different sort of transport. Alison was teaching me to ride.

Her method was to saddle a horse for me, mount her own, then gallop away at great speed. My horse, anxious not to be left behind, would rush to catch up, giving her the oppor-tunity to turn in the saddle and shout corrections and comments on my style.

Riding was something all the Yabsleys did extremely well. Even Mabel, in the brief intervals between childbearing, had ridden with her family. The boys had always ridden ponies to the grammar school in Kingsbridge, because their father would not pay bus fares. They would take the old coach road which led them past Collapit and Blanks Mill creeks, and brought them out by the cattle market. The ponies were stabled at the Seven Stars, at the foot of the steep hill which is Kingsbridge Fore Street. At fifteen, Charles had been appren-ticed as a jockey, but he grew too heavy to make it his career.

There were still a few horses left at Beadon; Lion, the big

shire, still used to pull a cart and to pull the tractor out when it got stuck in the mud; Peggy, their father's black mare; Rocket, who I think was Peggy's offspring; Strawberry, a heavy cob; and two Dartmoor ponies, Goldilocks and Pippin belonging to Francis' ten-year-old daughter Annabel (who rode like a cowboy).

I was usually given Strawberry, because he was considered good-natured and reliable, though he did alarm me once, when we were riding on North Sands, by continuing to wade into the water until he was out of his depth and striking out with the apparent intention of swimming across to Portlemouth on the far side of the estuary. He did decide to head back to the beach, with me, but without my boots.

The caravan site was growing into a lucrative business, large enough to need full-time management and to begin to worry the local council. In the summer, Alison was kept busy with caravanners coming to the kitchen door to collect keys and mail and to buy the cream, which she separated from the milk brought in in the mornings by Francis. Many people had been coming to Beadon for years and had become family friends. They were brought into the kitchen and given coffee and home-made fruit buns and, very often, errands to run for Mabel.

It also fell to Alison's lot to clean the newly erected toilets, and to collect the rents from the campers. This she did as a sideline to caring for her mother, keeping the chickens and running the enormous farmhouse with clockwork efficiency.

At the end of his South African tour, Charles had only three years to serve in the navy before retiring with a pension at forty. He saw the caravan site as a possible future career and was keen to see it develop. He had plans to terrace the steep fields at the top of the hill and to lay in lines for water and electricity.

As the summer progressed, it demanded more of his free time. He got into the habit of going straight to Beadon when he returned from Devonport in the early afternoon, and staying till ten or eleven at night on the site, levelling caravans, changing gas cylinders and generally bringing aid and cheer to an appreciative and adoring public. He admitted that it was a bit tough for me, but pointed out that the season lasted only twelve, or at the most, fourteen weeks.

So I waited and learned to cope with my loneliness, filling my days in making the cottage bright, cleaning and polishing and bringing in flowers from the woods, trying to turn myself into what I thought he wanted as a wife.

I was a little afraid of him at first. He never hit me. I was the one who lashed out when he goaded me beyond endurance, but his rages and his sneering sarcasm were things to be dreaded. He would enter the house in the manner of a ship's captain doing his rounds and find something I had failed to do; a record left out of its sleeve or a comb left on a window ledge. It became clear to me quite soon that I could not please him. No matter how I polished and cleaned, I would never be Alison's equal as a cook/housekeeper and would, therefore, always be her inferior as a woman.

Charles had known many women, apart from his mother and sisters, but only carnally. He was honestly astonished to discover that a love of cooking and an urge to provide personal valeting services were not part of the genetic make-up of the human female.

From an early age, the Yabsley girls were expected to help in the house and to wait on their father and brothers. True, the boys had to dig dock-weeds out of the fields and give a hand with the milking, but no one thought it unnatural when they complained or tried to dodge these chores.

One of Alison's jobs as a little girl had been to polish her father's leather gaiters. As a woman, she continued to clean the shoes of any of her brothers who happened to be staying in the house. She also put a freshly laundered shirt on Charles' bed each morning, with the collar stud and cuff links already in place. His shining shoes she placed in the centre of his bedside rug, laces loosened, with clean socks beside them.

She did this to buy herself a little peace in the mornings. It prevented a lot of rampaging and door slamming if everything he needed was to hand. I didn't appreciate this at the time and absolutely refused to clean his shoes. It was an issue between us for a long time.

Charles had been home for about a year when his mother announced that she was going to marry her old friend Richard Jackson, who had retired some years earlier from farming neighbouring Horsecombe.

The family received the news with some hilarity, but were generally pleased. Dick Jackson had always been held in high regard in the district and had received an OBE for his work when the American forces took over the South Hams in preparation for the Normandy landings.

Charles was not completely delighted. He didn't much care for the idea of a stepfather, though that was not his chief concern. He saw that it meant the end of a way of life that he had loved. There would be no more noisy family gatherings on Sunday nights, when he, brother Richard and Alison huddled round the table, smoking and trying to outdo each other in a cut-throat game of canasta, the only interruption permitted being when May and I served the huge pasties Alison had earlier placed in the oven.

After Mabel's departure to live in Kingsbridge, Alison didn't want to remain alone in the farmhouse and looked around for a live-in job. She answered an advertisement for a housekeeper in the *Western Morning News*, placed by a bank manager whose wife had died suddenly from viral pneumonia, leaving a ten-year-old child.

Her exceptional qualities were recognised and she got the job. Within a couple of months, Peter, her employer, offered her a more permanent contract and, less than a year after her mother's wedding, she too was married.

Beadon farmhouse could not be left unoccupied, so Charles and I moved in, with the only addition to our family we had so far managed to acquire: Simon, my boxer puppy.

Once or twice during that summer, when there had been a double-booking on a caravan, or some other minor disaster befell, like a collapsing tent, Hangar Mill was let to visitors, who rapidly removed any vestige of the polish I had so pain-stakingly applied.

I never seemed to see Charles alone, except when he finally came to bed. There was always someone at his heels. One or more young men followed him about, apparently simply to bask in the glow of his personality, or maybe just to see what he would do next. I thought of them as his puppy dogs. I was not resentful of all of them, some I got to know well enough to become a friend.

One morning, Charles brought home a young couple and their three small children, introducing them as John and Angela Yeoman. They were staying in a caravan, though not at Beadon, but at cousin Paul's Moult Farm, on the south side of North Sands Valley. John was a big, square man, as sound and solid as the chunks of rock he dug from his quarry in Somerset. Angela was, is, a small, dynamic redhead. The two men had found a rich seam of friendship and Charles, as was his habit, was soon deep in discussion about the future of Beadon now that his mother and Alison were settled.

For once, he had chosen his confidants well. John and Angela were both level-headed entrepreneurs, whose skills were already transforming the small, run-down quarry John had inherited from his father, into a huge international company. They were interested to hear about Beadon. Over the next few weeks, between the three of them, they worked out a scheme to buy out Charles' brother and sisters and, together, they set about trying to raise the capital.

The proposition, when put to the family, stirred up the kind of sibling warfare not witnessed since the sons of mediaeval monarchs bumped each other off in order of seniority. I grew weary of the endless circular arguments that raged whenever two or more of them were together, to which they all made heated contributions, though none listened. Their squabbling drove me mad. The only way I could keep my equilibrium, was to leave the house and seek fresh air and solitude.

I hadn't been feeling quite well for some time. I had lost a lot of weight, then, one morning, driving to Plymouth with Charles, I had to ask him to stop so that I could be sick in the hedge. It dawned on me. Catherine was signalling her embryonic presence.

About this time, Charles was asked to go to Exeter to meet some officials of the county council, to discuss the future development of the caravan site. They put it to him, that it would be altogether more desirable to move the whole site farther down the hill, nearer the sea, where it would be less visible than in its present position, which could be seen for miles around. But the idea was dismissed. The family had already invested a good deal of money in levelling plots for individual vans, laying in water pipes and in the new lavatories. They were not willing to see this money wasted.

A few days before Charles and John Yeoman were to sign contracts to purchase the land, the council dropped its bombshell. They designated the four camp-site fields as an area for housing development, sending the value sky-high and beyond the reach of John and Charles.

It was not long before a developer bought the farm and soon the caravans were replaced by rows of houses, the steepness of the land ensuring that each one was clearly visible from more than three miles away. Most were built with a blind side turned towards that glorious view down Beadon Valley.

6

Sailor Turns Entrepreneur

Any girlish fantasy I might have had about royal treatment while I was 'with child' evaporated when I told Charles of his impending fatherhood. He received the news with: 'About bloody time', and turned his attention to the liver I had bought for supper. It was the wrong kind of liver. Pig's, when it should have been lamb's, or the other way round. Either way, he was very displeased and cursed and slammed about the house before departing for the Fortescue sharp at nine o'clock.

I reflected, as I washed the dishes, trying to keep my nostrils closed against the nauseous smell of fried onions, that he really did have a raw deal. It would have been much better if he had married the daughter of the neighbouring farmer who had had her eye on him for years. She would have known which liver to buy and might have shared his view of childbirth as something that cows and sheep accomplish without drawing attention to themselves, requiring at most, only a handful of straw thrown down in a corner. Having grown up on a farm, her attitudes would be more robust than mine. She would have witnessed, as Charles had, the way farmers dealt with birth and its after-effects. He had seen his father treat a ewe with uterine prolapse by pushing the offending organ back into place, making small slits with his penknife in the flaps of skin on either side of the vaginal opening and simply tying the edges together with a bit of binder twine. It was effective and the beast didn't complain.

When Alison astonished the family and shoved me firmly from the limelight by announcing, only two weeks later, that she too, was pregnant, she displayed the same earthy acceptance. While I continued to throw up after every mouthful, her appetite for food and fags remained undiminished. She bustled about, slapping my drooping back whenever she saw me, saying, 'When the apple's ripe, he'll drop.'

I had learned about excessive vomiting in pregnancy as a student nurse. It was not understood why it should afflict some women and not others, but one theory was that it demonstrated a sub-conscious urge to be rid of the foetus. I could not accept this, since I looked forward to my child. My doctor never named my condition (hyperemesis gravidarum), or confirmed that I had it, but I suspected it. I was treated with Largactil, which did nothing to control the sickness and increased the already powerful urge to sleep the whole time; so I didn't take it.

One evening, towards the end of the fifth month, I went to bed early, having spent longer than usual peering into the porcelain pan groaning, 'Baby, why are you doing this to me?' I was surprised by the doctor coming into the room. Charles had sent for him.

He sat on the bed and we discussed the matter. He thought I might have a grumbling appendix and, as he didn't want to take the chance of the thing becoming acute in the middle of labour, when the pain would be attributed to the pangs of birth, with possibly disastrous consequences, he proposed sending me to hospital that night, for investigation.

Two days later my appendix was removed, though it was another four months before I could examine my scar without the aid of a mirror.

John Yeoman and Charles made several more attempts to set up in business together, but they came to nothing. The old cinema on the corner of Church Hill and Fore Street came on the market and Charles had ideas for running it along the lines he had seen in South Africa, where the clients watched the films while being served dinner in a pleasant dining-room. Searches revealed that the county council had plans to pull it down to make lorry access to the town easier. This they did in due course, taking another chip off the essential character of the place in the dreaded name of 'rationali-sation'.

Charles and John looked at the Moult when its owner, Lady Clementina Waring, died, with a view to turning it into a hotel. There are probably lovely houses in settings just as beautiful, elsewhere in the world, but none can be more beautiful. It stands amid woodland on a small green promon-tory between North and South Sands, looking out to the famous sand-bar which stretches across the entrance to the harbour. Lawns slope away from pink walls to the cliff top in front and to rock-strewn beaches on either hand. I was quite glad when they decided the conversion would be too costly and the question of what Charles would do when he left the navy was shelved for the moment.

We returned to live at Hangar shortly before probate was granted on James Yabsley's will and Charles received his portion of the estate. I fought and won a battle to have the house connected to the mains water supply. I had been content with water piped from the spring until, after a dry spell, a slow-worm had squeezed its way out of the tap and roused fears about the health of the coming baby. Charles objected on the grounds that his tea wouldn't taste the same, but gave in to surprisingly little force.

My daughter was born at the end of April, after a labour so protracted that the midwife and I both regretted that I chose to stay at home, but at last, at the end of a rough voyage, the passenger was safely in my arms. That night, Charles grilled for me a halibut, the like of which I have not tasted since.

The first summer of Catherine's life was like all Salcombe summers for me, even wet ones, full of light, colour and new faces. Regular visitors returned and for a few weeks assumed ownership of the streets and harbour. Those coming for the first time claimed an exciting discovery. The locals, in the pubs, beavering at bed-and-breakfasts, and grafting in the shops and hotels, welcomed them and the money they brought and waited for the winter to get their town back.

Some new faces came to stay. Little shops and boarding houses changed hands. Geoff and Joan Ware gave up their jobs in Birmingham and invested their all in one of the imposing houses on the hill above the Moult, to launch into the hotel business. The Yeomans dumbfounded the locals by paying more than £5,000 for a weekend cottage on the narrow quayside, where children fished for crabs and, in the summer, had swimming lessons from William Hannaford, the butcher. William taught several generations of Salcombe children to swim by dangling them over the wall at high tide in a canvas loop held by a boat hook.

A few yards away, at the entrance to Batson Creek, Richard Cove lived in the elegant Island House with his elderly mother, Lily. The house adjoined the family boatyard run by the youngest of Lily's three sons, Edward. Richard, the middle one, was skipper of the crabbing boat *Newbrook*. The eldest, John, had chosen to make his life away from Salcombe and came only as a visitor. Like Hangar, these houses were permanently open to friends. Charles' circle of friends was wide but he, Richard and John Yeoman became almost blood brothers. At weekends or whenever they could get together the three, frequently joined by John's friend Jim Cox and whoever Charles had magnetised in the pub, would go carousing round Devon. Usually they had a mission, devised by Charles, to find a water-wheel, a pony trap or a petrol-driven generator. It involved exploration of outlying farms and villages and required frequent stops for refreshment.

Wives joined them when they could. Sometimes on summer evenings, when the tides were favourable, we would take an open boat from Cove's yard, and motor up the estuary to visit a pub in Kingsbridge or at the head of South Pool Creek. Timing was crucial. It was essential to start on a rising tide, spend the time of slack water in the bar and get back to the boat before the tide turned. Mistiming could mean eight hours marooned on the mud.

On one such trip, we left our return later than was wise. Richard, knowing the local waters best, was standing in the stern, the tiller between his knees; John was peering into the deepening darkness for the channel markers when he remarked in his quiet, measured way that he thought we were about to run aground because he could see a seagull on the water up ahead that appeared to be standing on the bottom. 'The water', he said, 'is just above its ankles.'

Richard got us back to deep water, the little incident forgotten in the enchantment of gliding over the glassy water between banks of trees crowding to the edge; of watching phosphorescent bubbles leap after a trailing hand; and of rounding the headland to see Salcombe resting like a jewelled coronet on the dark velvet of the estuary.

Visitors often asked what we found to do in the winters. For me, they were never long enough. I loved my solitary evenings by the fire, the peace after the bustle of summer. We often went in a group to Plymouth to see a film or to a restaurant. We almost never went anywhere alone.

The annual Hunt Ball at the Salcombe Hotel drew everyone socially inclined from the whole area, though the same faces tended to turn up at every event. It was the peak of the Christmas party season. Despite its title, few attenders had ever hunted and though the local upper-middle classes were well represented, they mixed as happily in the ballroom with dinner-jacketed dustmen, boatmen and plumbers as they did in the pubs, where they all wore jerseys, jeans and Wellington boots.

One year, as we were mounting the stairs from the ballroom to go home, a well-lubricated Charles spotted a publican friend from Kingsbridge whom he considered to be homosexual, going up in front of us. The term 'gay' had not yet been coined. 'Happy New Queer!' he shouted. His friend spun on the stair and, without replying, punched him accurately in the eye.

With the end of his naval career looming and me pregnant again, finding a job for Charles became pressing. He considered everything that didn't involve leaving Salcombe, which limited the choice considerably.

It was 1961, the year of Dr Beeching, British Rail's mad axeman. The railway had never come closer than Kingsbridge and now the line was to close. The small cottage in Fore Street, used by BR as a parcels office, was advertised in the *Gazette* for tender. Charles submitted a proposal for a restaurant and was granted a twenty-one-year lease.

It was a typical Devon village cottage. Double fronted, a passage running through the centre from front to back doors; two rooms on either side of the passage; a staircase running up between the two rooms on the left giving access to four bedrooms above. Each room, above and below, had a small iron fireplace. The back door opened on to a grassy yard where there were several sheds. A high brick wall stretched across the far end, cutting off the view of the estuary which washed its outer side. We both thought it had potential.

Charles set about the conversion with manic enthusiasm. He rounded up every tradesman in the town and started gutting the place. Easter was five months away and he intended to be open. He took out so many fireplaces and internal walls that Gordon Rothwell, the town surveyor, became alarmed and insisted on jacks being put in to hold up the roof.

He had very clear ideas about the restaurant he wanted. It was to be modelled on Rules in Maiden Lane, Covent Garden, where diners sit in curved, red plush banquettes. He found three Polish shopfitters in Plymouth to build them for him and to make the round oak tables. He was bold and imaginative, ordering the best of everything, not pausing to count the cost.

Among his current band of followers were several future members of staff. One of them, hearing him refer, in nautical style, to the kitchen as the galley, suggested that that should be the name; and so it came about.

The estimated opening day of Good Friday, which fell at the end of April that year, was over optimistic, as such estimates always are. The Galley was nearing completion, but had some way to go. The alcoves and tables were in place, a side-lamp with a silk shade between each, the mosaic floor laid and a garden running down to the water had replaced the scruffy yard. Some suppliers of the kitchen equipment which he had ordered from the London Catering Exhibition failed to meet their promised delivery dates and opening day had to be postponed.

It so happened that my second child, with a sense of the dramatic, chose to begin his entrance on that Good Friday. I had planned to have him at home and arranged for a girl to stay in the house to look after Catherine, who was not quite two.

As labour progressed it became clear that this birth was going to be as drawn out as Catherine's and the doctor ordered me into hospital. Charles was extremely agitated. The ambulance was bumping its way along the back lane when the telephone rang. The huge cooking range had arrived from the Midlands and wouldn't go through the door. I just had time to shout instructions about fetching my mother from where she was living in Newton Abbot, before he hurtled away.

Stephen was born on Easter Saturday. When Charles came to see me in the evening, I kept drifting off to sleep, but I saw him look down at the baby and a smile light his eyes. He was pleased. He felt in his pocket and brought out a jeweller's box.

'Here,' he said: 'This is for you.'

Surprised by the romantic gesture, I opened it. Inside I found a wide, silver bangle.

'Frank Richardson sent it to you,' Charles went on, 'I gave his boy your MG. This is a swap.'

When Lil came the next day, I was more alert, but she seemed strained and had completely lost her voice. Excitement, she said, when she heard the news. It seemed odd, since this was her third grandchild. She didn't want to worry me, but there had been a terrible row with Charles the night before and he had thrown her out of the house. Catherine was OK.

I arranged to go home immediately, glad in any case to be with Catherine. I went to bed and Charles took the girl off for a lunch-time drink. Not for many years did my mother tell me that she had caught them in bed together the night Stephen was born.

The Galley opened on 2 June. The first weeks were chaotic with Charles trying to satisfy every sector of the market by serving breakfast, morning coffee, hamburgers, pasties, lunches, cream teas and dinner. It soon became clear that its slot was up-market, serving mainly the local fish and shellfish. He was fortunate in his chef. Hazel Whittaker came to live in the rooms above the restaurant with her two school-age children and established the restaurant's reputation for 'outstandingly good food', and 'cooking much above average', to quote the guides of the time. The Galley had many good chefs but none ever excelled her.

Superb cooking and lovely surroundings brought the customers flocking, but there is no doubt that what kept the place packed every night from door to door was the personality of the host. To define what I once heard ironically described as Charles' elusive charm is impossible. A man totally without reserve, he didn't recognise it in others. It gave him a disarming, often startling directness. Social barriers were no problem to him; he just didn't see them. His manner was the same whether he was greeting a coalman or a count; he was genuinely pleased to see them.

Women customers were treated with a degree of respect. Most were kissed as they came in and called 'Darling' for the duration of the evening, which pleased a good many of them, especially those who hadn't heard the endearment applied to them for a number of years. He was good at sensing when this approach would be unwise, though he did come unstuck occasionally. Heavily ringed hands were pressed to his lips with a murmured threat to cut them off.

He was once handed a cheque in payment for a meal, by a young, good-looking man with long hair. The signature and printed name were one word; one of the Midlands counties.

'Is that Mr Denbigh?' asked Charles.

'No, Lord Denbigh,' came the reply.

'You don't look much like a bloody lord to me.'

It peeved him that I didn't do more to help in the restaurant. Pointing out that I had two babies and a large house, which was now used as a boarding house for a number of young waitresses, didn't impress him. His mother, he said, had seven and still managed to raise the chickens and do the milking. He took to bringing home the tablecloths for laundering. Added to the nappies and the household washing, it meant that my two long clotheslines were permanently full. I rebelled and refused to do the tablecloths.

He liked to eat at home, though I had no interest in cooking and produced results far inferior to Hazel's. Sunday lunch was as much a requiem for his father as a family meal. The carving knife, fork and steel were laid beside his place at the head of the table. When the children and any guests were assembled, when the vegetable dishes, which had to include fluffy boiled rice, were put on the table beside a jug full of gravy thick with onions, he was ready to have the joint placed before him. Every week, I waited and he never failed. As he pierced the meat with the carving fork, he would ask, 'Where did you buy the meat?'

He did not require a reply since there was only one butcher in Salcombe. I tried to vary my answers, sometimes saying I'd had it flown in from Argentina or I'd nipped up to Harrods' food hall. It didn't matter, he could go on to the next stage of the ritual, which was to pronounce it over- or under-done. In eighteen years, I never once got it quite right.

7

Ordeal by Marriage

It seemed we had struck gold with the Galley. Salcombe, in 1962, boomed like the rest of the country. People could afford two or even three holidays. Second-home owners came every weekend and crammed the harbour with their pleasure cruisers, competing for space with visiting yachts. The restaurant buzzed with diners happy to wait, often till the early hours, to get their food. Charles worked unceasingly without actually involving himself in the manual labour of running the place; a trick he learned in the navy.

It was natural that he should regard his little domain as a ship. Fifteen minutes before opening for the evening session, he would do his 'Captain's round'. Grace, the sweet-faced local girl who was his head waitress, always left some small fault for him to find; a cigarette stub in an ash tray or a table wanting a pepper pot. The subsequent flow of blistering insults and bellowing subsided when the time came to open the door. Satisfied, he radiated geniality for the rest of the evening.

He did not cook, clean, man the bar or concern himself with keeping accounts, and apart from fetching and overseeing supplies, spent his time and energy on being a unique and quite superb 'front man'. The one gruesome job he could not delegate was disposing of the huge volume of rubbish generated every night. The local council removed a fraction of it but the remainder had to be loaded into a minivan and taken to an official tip.

It was distressing for Charles. He retched and gagged throughout the whole process, even though most of the waste was wrapped in black plastic. The sight of a chicken carcass set his stomach heaving. It gave the staff a great deal of amusement, but in one of our rare moments of communication he confided that it always revived a terrible memory for him.

In the early days of the war, when he was barely out of his teens, his ship had been sailing in convoy when one of the accompanying vessels was fatally hit. It was ablaze and threatening to blow up at any instant. Men were jumping overboard and swimming towards them, when Charles' commanding officer made a godlike decision. Faced with the choice of picking survivors from the water, or coming alongside the stricken ship long enough for the greater number of men still on board to jump to safety, he chose to bring his own ship alongside. The men in the water were crushed between the two.

I have wondered since, whether, had I known the little I know now about post-traumatic stress syndrome, I might have understood his behaviour better and been able to forgive his persecution of me.

Just before the start of our second season, Charles was invited by some naval friends to go as a guest of the wardroom on a month's cruise to Barbados. One of the girls who worked at the Galley came to stay with me to help with the children, releasing me to look after the restaurant.

I wasn't surprised to find a pile of unopened mail, there was a similar one at home. Charles believed that if you left it for long enough, by the time you got round to opening it, most of it was out of date and could be thrown away. This proved to be true, but there were a number of unpaid bills requiring urgent attention. The discovery that there was nothing in the bank to meet them was a shock.

Asking where all the money I had seen passing through the till had gone was futile. All I could do was gather in what money was owing to us and send out promises to pay at Easter, when trade picked up, those debts that couldn't be dealt with immediately. This was in fact the system that Charles learned from his father. It was customary for farmers to meet at the market to buy stock and implements and part with a handshake and a promise to pay on the next quarter day. Debts were always honoured as Charles always honoured his; eventually.

When Charles returned from the cruise, John Yeoman persuaded him and me that I should look after the money. I had no expertise, but even with my fear and loathing of all things arithmetical, I was the best person for the job, since if anything were to go astray, it at least strayed in the right direction.

I was enjoying my babies and didn't want to entrust their care to someone else, even for part of the time, but handing over the housework gave me no qualms at all. John sent a little hand-operated adding machine to help and encourage me.

The idea of having a Continental-style Mamma keeping a grip on the family fortune appealed to Charles and he agreed. A firm of stocktakers was brought in and their agent taught me the rudiments of bookkeeping and cash control. I also worked in the bar on three or four nights a week, to keep a better eye on the till.

We never did get the business on firm ground. The tremendous gains we made in the summer drained away in the winter. I sided with the bank manager and the accountant in urging that we close from November to March, but Charles wouldn't hear of it. He felt a deep obligation to his local customers and to the people he employed. I could not prevail against him in this or any other matter. I took charge of the paying but not the spending, for which I received neither payment nor praise.

The Galley became the regular venue for charity events and fund-raising coffee mornings; coffee provided by

Charles. He also hosted an annual dinner for the old people of the town. His prominence and popularity increased and when he stood in the elections for the Salcombe Urban District Council, he got in with a huge majority.

Our house, nestling in a fold of hills, at the end of a dirt track, was as busy as Paddington Station. The comings and goings of people keen to be in Charles' company went on all day, easing only when the restaurant opened at night and they pursued him there.

In the middle of our third season, I came downstairs one morning and booted out a couple of young men I found curled up in sleeping bags on the dining-room floor. I didn't particularly want witnesses to my departure for the maternity hospital later that day in preparation for Lorna's birth on the next.

Winters were better, except for fine Christmas Days, when the stream of pre- and post-lunch callers left me with barely enough time to get my own turkey in the oven. I prayed every year for a wet Christmas.

Fewer customers off-season meant Charles sometimes got home around one in the morning, when he liked to start cooking. Like an actor finishing a demanding performance, he was too wound up to go straight to bed. Bursting into the bedroom as though it were one in the afternoon, he'd ask if I'd like some scallops grilled in the shell with breadcrumbs, or perhaps some tasty sweetbread. I usually agreed, as when I didn't he brought them up to me anyway.

We didn't open on winter Sunday evenings. May and Richard and, usually, my parents, who by now were living in Salcombe, came over for a cold supper. Richard and Charles played noisy games of cards or draughts, their affection for each other not easy to discern behind the arguments and the crowing and gloating of the winner.

Council duties and the business kept him away from home for most of the day, which allowed us to work out a method for an uneasy co-existence. In the morning, in volatile temper, he went to the Galley early to clear the rubbish, returning for a breakfast of bacon, eggs, fried potatoes and, very often, hog's pudding. There followed at least an hour of telephoning suppliers and fellow councillors, then back to the Galley and home again around three, his mood sweetened by light ale and several triumphs in the game of spoof. At six, or earlier if Tom and Jerry were on TV, I woke him from his afternoon sleep. The forty-five minutes before I saw him, with profound relief, leave again for the restaurant, were always a most savage and dangerous time, which had to be negotiated with the greatest care.

Another woman might have managed him better. I could not bring myself to use 'feminine wiles' to deceive and manipulate him to keep the upper hand. He would have been an easy enough subject and even if he'd suspected, he would have accepted it as normal interplay between man and wife. His mother had resorted to the most amazing feats of cunning to extract money from his father. He laughed whenever they were recalled.

Not for me. It stuck in my throat to have to ask for anything and a refusal left me burning with resentment. If I dyed his shirts pink or shrunk a sweater in the wash, as I did fairly often, I didn't try to conceal it, but learned to endure the carping and complaining which could last for weeks. I even began to take a perverse delight in watching him rave when I told him I'd made a bonfire of some of his old clothes, or failed to re-order the bottled gas for the cooker.

Our relationship deteriorated to the point when we could not work together. I gave up working in the bar and instead relieved him on two or three nights a week, managing the floor of the restaurant. We took to passing each other in doorways. As he came in, I went out. I did once suggest divorce, to which he replied that I could fuck off any time I liked, but not to imagine I could take the children with me. It wasn't an option I could consider and I lacked the initiative or courage to take any other.

At my instigation, and spurred by his terror of an impending journey by air, he made his will in favour of the children. In the event of his death I was to have a life interest in his estate or until I remarried. Richard and I were to be executors with a friend who was a solicitor in a Kingsbridge practice. It followed very closely the model of his father's will.

As Chairman of the Council, Charles was appointed Justice of the Peace. He took the position very seriously, if not all the cases that came before him on the bench. He was inclined to take a kindly view of motoring offences and misdemeanours committed while the offender, who was often someone he had known since boyhood, was drunk, caused him problems in keeping a properly solemn countenance. Fellow magistrates gave him sound guidance and restrained him from sucking bullseyes while the court was in session.

I became interested in local government and was elected to the Council, though I had a much tougher fight than Charles. I was defeated at my first attempt and got my seat at a by-election, having first to convince the electorate that I had made adequate childcare arrangements. No woman had ever served on their council before. For two years I worked on various committees, then I followed Charles as chairman, though automatic appointment to the bench had ceased by then.

A succession of 'mother's helps' came to live-in at Hangar. Few of them stayed for long, lured away by better employment or simply stolen to become Galley girls. The children adapted, enjoying a rare degree of freedom, with fields for their ponies, a stream on which to paddle a canoe, animals of every kind and a sandy beach at the end of the lane. Charles bought an old van from the travelling farrier and they all learned to drive, in a field, long before their teens.

I felt very strongly that none of them was realising their potential at school. It was true, I thought, of large numbers of children, but mine were the only ones I could do anything about and, despite our financial problems, I planned for each in turn to go away to school. Childhood and education cannot be postponed until business picks up.

Ballet classes had been an important element in the girls' lives. They were fortunate to be taught by the remarkable Elizabeth Schooling and both showed considerable aptitude, though less than that of one or two star pupils who gained entry to the Royal Ballet School.

When Catherine was still unhappy after a year at the local comprehensive school, I arranged for her to be auditioned at Elmhurst Ballet School, in Surrey. No one believed me, but I wasn't nurturing dreams of seeing a daughter dancing at Covent Garden; I simply thought she would enjoy, and benefit from, an arts-based education.

I drove her to the audition with my face plastered in concealing make-up, to cover a black eye; my own fault, I hit him first. This possible drawback did not stop her getting a place in the school the following September.

Charles was as miserable as I was at her going away from home, but he didn't oppose it too fiercely. The tradition in his father's family of leaving land to the sons and educating daughters so that they could marry well, made him more receptive to the idea than he might otherwise have been.

The latest reorganisation of local government had brought in a three-tier system, so that there was now to be, below county level, a much larger South Hams District Council based in Totnes. Salcombe was to become a parish council. After six years, I decided not to stand for re-election and to find another outlet for my energies, though where was difficult to know.

Charles was elected to Devon County Council. It increased the pressure on him and did nothing to sweeten his disposition. The volume of reports and written material relating to council affairs that dropped on the mat became so huge that it would have occupied full-time a person with nothing else to do. Every day saw him driving long distances to committee or council meetings. He cared passionately about local affairs, particularly anything that might affect the environment.

Morning telephoning sessions extended to two or three hours, when all housework had to be suspended because any noise or clatter sent him into a fury. He sat, jockey-like, with his feet hooked round the rung of the carver chair which stood against the wall in the dining room, filling a large ash tray as he talked endlessly of 'plenary powers' and 'standing orders'.

Hangar had changed quite a bit in our years of occupation. An extension had been added to the back of the house where it adjoined the mill and one of the smaller barns had been demolished and the barnyard levelled and made into a large lawn from where we could see the sea.

Restoration of the mill was still a cherished dream and whenever he could, Charles took a complete day off to continue his quest for a water-wheel of the right type and dimensions. The original had been a massive twenty feet in diameter, fed by an overshoot, the wheel being powered by water flowing over its paddles at the top of their circuit.

A remote farm in north Devon finally yielded one and, ever confident that the next season would be brilliant and wipe out all his money worries, he bought it and had it carted home in numbered bits. It was placed on top of the huge iron cover-plate of the reservoir beside the mill, to wait for the day of re-erection.

It never came. The beginning of the end of our peculiarly separate but parallel lifestyles came one day with a telephone call. I was upstairs, busying myself with some of the quieter chores, when Charles appeared in the doorway, looking strained and odd.

'Richard's dead,' he said in a strangled voice.

'Richard?' I was stupefied. His stutter had gripped him and he had to force it out.

'Brother Richard.'

We drove at once to be with May. Richard, without warning, had suffered a coronary thrombosis during the night and had died at her side. During the course of the day other members of the family joined us.

His funeral service was held in Stokenham Church from where, according to his wishes, he was taken for cremation. Observing another family tradition, no women attended this part of the proceedings.

May was at a loss to know which would be the most appropriate place to scatter the ashes. She liked my suggestion that they be strewn on the lawn at Hangar. It was a beautiful place that he had known and loved from childhood, on land that was still in the Yabsley name.

Some days later, a few of us gathered to scatter the ashes, say prayers and plant a memorial rose. The old buildings and the embracing hills gave a sense of peace and permanence. It seemed fitting at the time.

8

Reduced to Ashes

The Galley's staff were paid a little more generously in the summer because of the long hours and punishing pace of the work. In winter, pay packets reflected a survival strategy. The practice was generally, accepted as reasonable, most people regarding the seasonal rise as a perk. A few among the less mature took the opposite view and were incensed when the rate dropped. One such was a local boy taken on as washer-up late in the season. He bore his grievance through most of the following winter then, a few weeks after Richard's death in March, he got his revenge.

At around two, one morning, when Charles had been in bed for about half an hour, the neighbour who kept the greengrocery opposite the Galley phoned to tell him the restaurant was on fire. In a blind panic he dressed and rushed off. I could not go with him, there being no one in the house to stay with the children.

When he hadn't returned by breakfast time, I phoned and was told that he was still talking to the police. I went to fetch him, concerned that he had had no sleep, and stepped through the familiar front door into a stinking ruin.

The firemen had finished their work and were crunching in and out of a dark cavern, over the fragments of glass which covered the floor, packing up their equipment. The gloom and stench were deeply shocking. Ceiling tiles hung in black stalactites, bar shutters had twisted into grotesque shapes and bottles had either exploded or melted on the optics. Of the furnishing, pictures and ornaments, nothing remained. In the kitchen, only the range and a few pieces of crockery survived.

I found Charles sitting with two CID officers at one of the few tables untouched by the flames, near the door to the garden, where some light penetrated through a fanlight. The policemen didn't argue when I led him away. He was dirty and exhausted, hardly speaking on the way home except to tell me that the fire chief was certain it was arson. Three separate fires had been started by setting light to packets of paper napkins, one in the restaurant, one under the bar counter and another under a bed upstairs. This had failed to take hold, and there was little more than smoke damage to the first floor.

While I ran the bath, there was one call he felt he absolutely had to make; to the insurance assessor. The CID questioning had made him feel they suspected him of having started the fire himself. After that he sank into bed. The representative from the firm of loss adjusters was with us by midday, commenting that it was extremely unusual to be summoned by the victim, particularly so early in the morning.

During his examination of the building, he found a strand of red wool clinging to a back drain pipe, which he handed to the CID. Before the afternoon was out, the strand of wool had been matched to the socks still being worn by our young washer-up, who had also had a long spell without sleep, having spent the day watching the proceedings from the café opposite. He was one week short of his eighteenth birthday, the season two weeks short of Easter.

Confronted by a real disaster, Charles remained calm. In fact, the fire which destroyed his beloved Galley seemed to extinguish his own inner fire. For the first week, there was little he could do except oversee the clearing of the rubble. He came with me to collect Catherine for the Easter holiday, which was unusual. Then, with energy and enthusiasm he began to plan the rebuilding, but some vital force had gone from him.

Original thoughts of restoring the restaurant to the way it had been before the fire were discarded as soon as he realised what an opportunity he now had to extend to the sea wall, doing away with the garden. He could have a larger kitchen, more tables, more seating room in the bar. We were, of course, under-insured.

Of all the bitter losses he suffered, one he regretted most was that of the picture which had hung above one of the long tables. He had had it blown up from an old black and white postcard showing Salcombe from the Portlemouth side, taking in the ferry landing, small craft on the estuary and some of the old boat-building sheds along the foreshore.

A collection was started in the town to buy him a new picture. In a short time there was enough money to commission an oil painting from a renowned local artist and to make an enlarged reproduction of an old painting depicting Sharpitor and the harbour entrance.

Rebuilding went on all through the summer. When it was nearing completion, to add drama to the decor, Charles bought the mast of an old Thames barge that was breaking up on a beach, higher up the estuary. It was more than sixty feet long, much too tall to stand upright and six feet had to be sawn off before it could run the length of the dining room, supported on cross-beams at either end, just below the ceiling.

It had to be manhandled into place by ten of the strongest men to be found. Once there, I privately thought, it served no purpose other than to quietly pull the roof in, though it might be handy at Christmas as a fixture from which to dangle decorations.

Just before the reopening in August, I went to see how work was progressing. We stood together, looking down the elegant room which had replaced the garden, through the big window that formed the end wall, to where the sun glinted on the evening tide.

'It's beautiful,' I said. 'Really beautiful. You've got the restaurant you deserve.'

The tribute was sincerely meant and he seemed touched by it. He thanked me.

The arsonist was brought to trial at Exeter Crown Court in December. He pleaded not guilty, so his record was not made known to the court. Since he came from a local family, Charles knew that the boy had a history of fire-raising, and was probably the only person in the town with a heart generous enough to give him a job. The proper process of giving the accused the fairest possible hearing proceeded. Sitting in the public gallery, we listened as the defence listed all Charles' shortcomings as an employer and the reasons why the boy had felt provoked beyond endurance. Psychiatric reports showed that his mind was sound, though he had a 'personality defect'. The judge remarked that most people were similarly afflicted. He was found guilty and sentenced to a year in Borstal, from which the time spent on remand would be deducted. We left the court feeling we had been publicly flogged.

All through that wretched year, I had agonised over whether to respond to Catherine's pleas to bring her home and, finally, had given way. She started at a new school as a weekly boarder in the January term. On the last day of the Christmas holidays Charles took the children to Torquay to see a Disney film. He was a little more relaxed, happier now that Catherine was to be closer to home.

Two weeks into the term, on the morning of Wednesday, 22 January, he returned as usual at breakfast time. The other two children were at home, Lorna was sick and Stephen hadn't yet gone off to catch the school bus. He called to me from the bottom of the stairs. I paid not much attention at first; he always yelled for me if he didn't lay eyes on me immediately, being quite unable to bear being alone. A thing I cannot bear is to leave a job unfinished and I resolved to finish making the bed before I went down. When he shouted again, the note of panic in his voice made me abandon it and go to him.

I could see nothing to alarm me in his appearance, though he was breathless and wheezing as he did in times of great anxiety. He sank on to the sofa. 'Pains in my chest,' he said, 'Call the doctor.'

I phoned the doctor on call then attended to Charles. His colour was good, but he was distressed by lack of air. 'Leave the door open,' he said.

I opened wide the front door which led directly into the living room and let in the winter sun. He sat, not speaking, but seemed relieved by the cold breeze on his face. I sat beside him, my mind churning. My cleaning woman was due that morning and I knew I had to stop her coming at all costs. She was a chatterbox and was obliged to bring her particularly noisy and destructive two-year-old son with her to work. Not what Charles needed right now.

The doctor arrived, his presence calming and reassuring. An injection was given and he left, saying that there were arrangements to make. I sat beside Charles on the sofa, he was quiet, subdued, but breathing more easily. He'd be OK now.

The children were hovering anxiously about, I was worrying illogically about the untidy house and the unmade beds. I phoned the cleaning woman and got no reply. She must have already started walking down to Hangar from her house at the top of the hill. I felt desperately that I must head her off.

His arm was resting across my shoulders. I turned to him and explained that I was going to stop her coming, that I would be gone only a couple of minutes. 'All right, my sweetheart,' he said.

I made him more comfortable, putting his feet up and propping him up with cushions. 'Stephen,' I said, 'stay with your father till I get back,' and I went out, leaving him alone with the children. I didn't think he was going to die. I drove up the farm road until I met the cleaning lady coming down. I explained that Charles was ill and needed quiet. We would leave the work until tomorrow. I turned and hared home again. As I rattled over the bump in the drive formed by the roots of the hawthorn tree that grew half way down the path-field, I saw Stephen come running round the corner of the barn, waving his arms. I didn't stop to ask him questions, we rushed into the house together.

Charles had suffered another, more massive attack. He was lying unconscious, on his back, still breathing, but in deep convulsive gasps. I got through to the surgery.

'Please. You must come. You must come,' I shouted into the phone.

I motioned to Stephen to take his ashen-faced sister upstairs while I began to massage his chest, trying to keep him breathing. I pleaded, 'Don't die. Please don't die.'

I stood aside when the doctor, another of the partners, materialised behind me. He listened for a few minutes with his stethoscope, then shook his head. I was dumbstruck, then the doctor put his arms round me and I managed: 'How am I going to tell the children?'

'We have to tell them,' he said. 'We'll tell them together.'

They were sitting quietly together in my bedroom, wide-eyed and frightened. Stephen's face crumpled when he saw us coming, Lorna flung herself into my arms and clung to me sobbing. I held her and rocked her. I had no hand free for my silently weeping Stephen. It fell to the doctor to hug him. I did not cry. There was so much to be done. Ringing friends to bring Catherine home, telling his family. Suddenly my mother was there. The butcher had heard and brought her in his van. Connie, my sister, calling from Aberdeen said, without hesitation, that she would come. I clung to that as something solid and certain in a fearful future.

I decided not to have his body taken to a chapel of rest. He would not have wanted to be sent away from home. The doctor and the undertaker carried him up to the little bedroom at the top of the stairs. When the coffin arrived in the afternoon, it was placed on trestles between the beds.

I thought it better that Catherine should see his body, if she chose, so that she would accept as fact what she might otherwise have difficulty in accepting. The other two, to my eternal shame, had witnessed his death, alone.

The first of the two doctors returned to give me the signed death certificate. He also gave me some sleeping pills and pressed a banknote into my hand. I walked with him to the gate. He had been fond of Charlie. He looked down at me sadly: 'I don't know how we would have managed to lay him by the heels.'

When I woke next morning, I knew something momentous had happened, but for a moment couldn't remember what. Then it came to me. Charles is dead. It was unreal. Charles is dead. Then, unbidden and shocking, came another thought: 'I'm free.'

On Friday, his portrait smiled out at me from the front page of the *Salcombe Gazette*, news of his death making the front-page lead story. Soon, wreaths and flowers filled the house and overflowed into the alley outside the back door. Letters and cards arrived by the hundred, among them one from the producer of a TV programme in which Charles had taken part, asking my permission to go ahead with the trans-mission. I gave it, unwittingly stirring up a controversy in the letters pages of the local paper after the programme appeared, between people who were pleased to see it and those who thought it bad taste to show film of one so recently dead. Some letters were critical of the producer. I always meant to write to the paper myself, in his defence, but never got round to it; another reason for guilt.

Preparations went on for the funeral. Quantities of food were prepared for guests who would return to the house and, on the morning, as a gift, my hairdresser came to the house to do my hair. Shops in the town closed for the day.

The cortège looked weird against the background of the mellow old walls of the mill and barns. I felt I had been cast as lead player in an unrehearsed pageant. The coffin slid smoothly into the hearse, was covered in flowers and Charles began his last and slowest journey up across the pathfield. I followed with the children, noting how smart, small and vulnerable they looked.

The church was already full when we arrived, people filling the gallery and the body of the hall, with the exception of the seats reserved for the family. Throughout the service, I kept watch on the children, but they were composed and quiet. A woman about four rows behind me was weeping loudly. When we rose to leave, I tried to pick her out, but couldn't distinguish anyone in the ranks of faces. Walking out of church, we stepped into the centre of an amphitheatre. The steep streets were lined with people looking down on us. My sense of unreality expanded.

I sent the children home with my parents and some close friends, thinking the burial might be too much of an ordeal for them. I was concerned too at how weary my father seemed.

The headstone was in place at the top of the open grave. Earth was piled beside it on a green canvas, like blankets, I thought, folded back on a bed in readiness for the admission of a patient. The undertakers had been superbly efficient; so many details arranged without my having to worry. I read the embossed words on the headstone: Charles Yabsley, followed by dates of birth and death, then 'Beloved husband of Eunice'. Oh God! Had I agreed to that? Was it a sin to say such a thing when my heart felt cold as stone? 'Ah well,' I comforted myself. 'I certainly loved him once.'

Nowhere are there guidelines on the subject of how quickly bereaved children should return to school, but after a week, staying around the house all day didn't seem good for them, so I sent them back. We resumed ballet classes and Sea Scouts too. I planned to re-open the Galley on Saturday night, the second after Charles' death.

This was economic necessity. A review of my financial situation showed it to be grim. I already knew about the trade debts but the premiums on an insurance policy had lapsed, so a weekly income I had counted on would not be forthcoming, which was a bit of a body blow.

There were two options, sell the restaurant and stay on in the house, depending on social security and whatever work I could find. This would not pay for the ambitious plans I had for the children, or keep the buildings in decent repair. Running a car, essential when you live in rural isolation, would be beyond my means. The other option, sell the house and keep the Galley, emerged from my deliberations as the logical course. We would live over the shop. The children were no longer infants and having them and my work all under one roof solved the problem of how to be carer and breadwinner at the same time.

There began a series of visits to the solicitor, my only remaining co-trustee. Our families had always been friends, though not close friends. We knew each other quite well. When I first married Charles, I had toyed with the idea of joining the local amateur dramatic society in which the then young and handsome solicitor was a leading actor, but a certain amount of ridicule from Charles, then the arrival of Catherine, killed off the notion. I'd always rather regretted it.

My decision to carry on running the Galley presented him with a difficulty. As trustee, it was his duty to see the estate wound up satisfactorily. The simplest way to do that was to sell it, settle the debts and hand any residue to me. It would not, however, give me the seven years of high income that I needed. I was, I'm afraid, callously indifferent to anything but my own concern with survival.

On the Friday evening after the funeral, I was in my bedroom at Hangar, sorting through some papers which were kept in the old iron strong-box Charles inherited from his mother. I was holding the key, a large, ornate object, when my brother appeared in the doorway. Like my parents, he had moved permanently to the area and, for the last week, in my time of stress, he had been very attentive, so I was not surprised to see him.

'Sit down, I've got to tell you something,' he said.

I sat on my bed and waited.

'Dad's had a heart attack. They've taken him to Kingsbridge Cottage Hospital. He's quite bad.'

'When?'

'Last night, he didn't want anyone to disturb you.'

I thought I took the news calmly, my sense of detachment persisting, but when I looked down at my hand, the heavy iron key was bent, almost at a right angle. Strange, but there it was.

Mentally, I prepared myself for no customers to turn up at all on the Galley's re-opening night. It could never be the same without Charlie and I thought clients were quite likely to demonstrate their regret by staying away. It pleased me then, when I arrived at the restaurant, to see the sprinkling of bookings reasonable to expect on a Saturday in early February. Twenty-five to thirty covers.

There were eight of us working that night. In the kitchen, two cooking, one preparing sweets and salads and one washing up. I had toyed with the idea of serving behind the bar myself, but decided to bring in Judy and two waitresses to man the restaurant.

Many of the people booked proved to be old friends who greeted me warmly. Some who hadn't booked turned up as well. By around nine, a pleasant buzz of chatter filled the room and the staff and I were running about trying to give good service to rather larger numbers than we had anticipated.

The door swung open every few minutes to admit more people. I began to get a little anxious. Seating was no problem: the new dining room easily held seventy at one sitting, but it was rapidly filling and the two waitresses were hard pressed. I couldn't possibly turn anyone away. Some had travelled from Plymouth and Exeter. I sent a round of drinks through to the kitchen to try to keep the chef sweet-tempered.

One party of six were growing unhappy and disgruntled. They had waited too long between courses and we had run out of one of the dishes they wanted to order. The host was in a sour mood, despite my efforts to make amends. Towards the end of the evening, I met one of the women in the powder room. She was crying. 'I'm so sorry your evening's been spoiled,' I offered, 'I just wasn't ready for so many people.'

She gave me an odd look. 'I'm not crying for that. We thought Charlie was going to be here.'

My father, who of all people in my life, was the one who loved me most, could not have fallen ill at a worse time for me. Afternoons, when I should have been getting to grips with such matters as what percentage of turnover should be spent on wages; stock control and the proper mark-up for food and wines – all things that I would have to master if I was to run a successful business – had to be spent taking my mother to the hospital to visit him. I was ashamed that I should feel in the least grudging of my time, he had always given so unstintingly of his.

At first he was well enough to be interested in how I was coping. It pleased him, having been a fan of the breed all his life, that I had bought a red Volkswagen Golf. Probably it had been a rash thing to do in my precarious situation, but the big greedy car Charles had driven was in the garage for repair and my old Citroën, which I heartily loathed, had twice broken down on the school run. When an uncle of Charles' in America sent me 500 dollars, I arranged to trade them both in for one of the first small hatch-backs to appear on the market. It arrived minus its dip switch, but I was otherwise happy with it.

I promised to wheel Father out to the hospital car park to see it as soon as he was well enough, but he never did get well enough. As it became more obvious that he could not recover, I wished I could take him home to die at Hangar, but I was not free to nurse him and the house was to be sold.

Once the decision to sell Hangar had been made, other difficulties which in settled times might have seemed insurmountable, were easier to deal with. I enlisted friends to advise me on how to set about selling the house and animals and clearing the barns. Sometimes, help arrived without my asking. The odd little man from Social Security who had sorted out the muddle caused by the absence of wages records and National Insurance stamps when I first kept the Galley books, came to see me and filled in the claim forms for my widowed mother's allowance.

One piece of luck lifted my spirits when the couple who had recently acquired the bakery next to the restaurant, offered me the vacant flat above their shop. They were enlarging the small cottage on the waterfront across a cobbled yard from the bakery for themselves and their children. I hardly knew them but they had formed a friendship with Charles and during the rebuilding of the Galley, had allowed him to place a fire-escape door in their party wall, opening on to their yard.

I accepted the offer, gladly paying rent in advance. Some alterations had to be done; closing off a staircase inside the shop and installation of a new one to give access to the flat from the back of the building. I planned to cut an opening and place a slow-burning fire door between the flat and the rooms above the restaurant. Together they would make a spacious and pleasant home for me and the children.

It was an exciting prospect. Planning the decor and deciding which pieces of furniture to take from Hangar gave me something to think about apart from my problems. It was a great relief to know I would have a bathroom. How to fit one into the tiny space over the restaurant had occupied my mind a good deal. It was good to feel that in the midst of dismantling my old way of life, I could begin to build a new one.

9

A Crossword Romance

Only a few people had dined on that Thursday night in February, when John pushed open the Galley door and walked in to have a drink before going home. I had done my round of the lingerers to ensure they had all they needed and settled with the crossword on the long bench in the bar, from where I could say goodnight to customers as they left and could watch to make sure no drunks spilled in as the pubs turned out.

I glanced up as the lock clicked and, reassured, looked down again at the crossword, missing the full dramatic effect of the man in his dinner jacket and frilled evening shirt filling the doorframe. It was as he passed me on his way to the counter that I became aware of him. The neat feet, planted in a slow tread; a sway of the shoulders too slight to be a swagger, but pronounced enough to signal supreme self-confidence.

'A Campari soda, please,' he asked of Judy, as I came up to greet him, before turning to me and introducing himself. 'I'm John Allen, the new restaurant manager at the Marine; will you have a drink?'

'No thanks, I'd rather have coffee. Would you like some?'

I fetched a tray with three cups, poured coffee for him, Judy and myself and perched on the stool beside him.

We talked of home and family. He had, he said, spent a long time in hospital with a kidney problem. He'd needed a change and the job at the Marine, with a flat, was just what he and Pat had hoped for. He was busy building a breakfast bar in his spare time. Pat was looking for a part-time job now that the two kids had started at the infants' school. It was all working out very well, 'Though I'm really too old to have young children,' he added.

'How old?'

'Forty last birthday.' He had celebrated with a breakfast party of kedgeree, champagne and orange juice.

He told me about Monica, his first wife and the two sons he had not seen for eight years, when they were six and seven. I was at a loss to understand how a parent could bear not seeing his children, but he explained that it was better for the boys that the break should be clean and complete. I didn't agree, but, being often baffled by male reasoning and knowing many divorced fathers held the same opinion, I let it pass. We chatted until my running up and downstairs to bring coats and umbrellas for departing customers made sensible conversation difficult. I returned from one of these absences to find that he had hijacked my crossword. I peered over his shoulder but the hand holding the elegant silver pen was so large, when it went down to write it obliterated the grid. Nettled, I moved to his left side. From there I could still read the clues.

I studied his profile as we bent over the paper. Almost handsome, but not quite. He reminded me, I decided, of a Siamese tom cat. Muscular, sleek, slightly slit-eyed. He stayed until the last customer had gone and Judy was letting down the bar shutters. I saw him out, performed the closing-up ritual of locking doors and turning off lights and fans, then went to retrieve my car from the quay to drive home to Hangar. Outside the darkened house, I sat for a while, listening to the stream running to still my mind. The sense of unreality remained, but I felt more at peace. Tomorrow, the agent from Jackson Stops and Staffs was coming to value the property. It had to be faced.

Next morning, Lil was looking tired. The house, with the steep steps up to the kitchen, was aggravating her arthritis and the children had been squabbling. She was doing her valiant best but her thoughts were constantly with my father and she hadn't the strength to meet their emotional needs. I barely had time to see them. They were having to struggle through their bereavement without much help. Better if they went back to school and a little normality returned to their lives.

The man from Jackson Stops and Staffs made no comment about the condition of the drive down from the gate at the top of the field. Not worth explaining how Charles had started to harden the surface by pouring on it used frying oil from the restaurant. I had protested, but I'd had to concede that it seemed to be working. The bit in the middle where the roots of the little hawthorn tree, beloved by the green woodpecker, spread themselves across the path, had become quite smooth and hard. It had been his intention to continue up to the top and down to the bottom.

I didn't drag the man up to the top garden where Dad had tried to start a vegetable garden among the old cider-apple trees, despite warnings that the ground was too steep to retain water. I just pointed it out from the road.

Opening the door of the big top barn was a bit embarrassing, there was so much junk piled in there wherever the floorboards were sound enough to take the weight. Better not to mention Charlie's barn dances; all those people jumping up and down on rotting timbers. The lower barns and the lawn I could show with pride. The children had swept the cobbles clean and hung the pony-tack neatly along the beams. In front, the four flowering cherry trees I had planted the year before had taken a good hold, making a lovely frame to the view down to the end of the valley, where the sea rolled in, seemingly at eye level. I tried not to think of Richard's ashes, scattered here soon after the cherry trees were planted, when we had thought there would always be Yabsleys at Hangar

Mill. Another reason to feel guilty.

The man was most interested to hear about the ruined mill. The water-wheel Charles had carted at such terrible expense from north Devon lay in bits among the bracken on top of the reservoir. It would never be erected now. I took him across to the orchard to show him the old butter well, but the undergrowth had covered the place. The ground there was soggy and it was getting very cold so, stepping over the old lamp post which had lain long on its side, waiting for the day when it would stand to light up the garden, I led the way indoors. We had tea by the fire, when he'd seen the house. The man sipped thoughtfully then said, 'This is a job for *Country Life*. We'll advertise sale by auction. We'll aim for May. Can you be ready by then?'

An auction? I hadn't thought of that. May? Three months to dispose of the furniture, get rid of the junk in the barns and find homes for the ponies.

'Yes,' I said.

John came again the next Thursday; this time, he'd changed into a sweater and slacks, immaculate and perfectly colour co-ordinated. He had brought a copy of *The Times* saying he thought it time we graduated to a more difficult crossword. Between us, we finished them both.

Work on the flat over the bakery was going well. We were nearly ready to break through between the buildings. I had expected some opposition from the solicitor about this – every plan I made seemed to land him in some ethical dilemma – but when I explained on the phone, he laughed: 'What will you do if a building inspector comes round?'

'I'll push a wardrobe or something over the doorway.'

So, the thing was done, giving me a small bedroom for Stephen, a larger room for the girls to share, a kitchen and a pleasant living-room with a French window opening on to a paved, flat roof, from where we had access to the flat roof of the Galley, with its truly spectacular view of the estuary. My own room was a small partitioned section of one of the store-rooms over the restaurant, but it was perfectly adequate. The outside staircase was not yet in place, but once the doorway had been cut, that didn't matter too much. Wally Grimson did the decorating, tackling the job with such energy he had it done in a week. I counted myself very fortunate.

Six weeks into widowhood, I was enjoying a heady sense of freedom. One indulgence I permitted myself was to have my hair done twice a week, at the little salon in Folly Lane, a narrow passage leading from Fore Street to the water's edge. One bright morning, I came out of the hairdresser's to find John coming down the alley towards me. Perfectly turned out, in a pin-striped suit, he looked out of place, like an actor who had strolled on to the wrong set. I was glad to see him.

'I saw your car outside the Galley with the tailgate up, so I knew you couldn't be far away,' he said.

'That's in hope of keeping the traffic warden at bay, if I'm late. I'm going to shift it now anyway, I'm going to Cornwood to get some ducks.'

'How far's Cornwood?'

'About twelve miles, up on the edge of the moor.'

'Will you be back by twelve? I have to be back for lunch-time service.'

'I could be.'

'Can I come with you?'

My little Golf was the first he'd seen and he asked if he could drive. He was obviously skilful. I learned that he used to enjoy rally-driving when he was in the army in Cyprus. That was when he was still married to Monica.

'Why come so far for ducks?'

'I need a large quantity and I need them fresh. We try not to have anything frozen, except stuff like peas.'

'I thought you were a fish restaurant.'

'We are. But there's always someone in a party who doesn't like fish, and duck and steak are the most popular alternatives.'

'And the fish? Do you buy that locally?'

'Salcombe is a crabbing port, I get crabs and lobster from here and Beesands, wherever I can get them, they're not plentiful like they used to be. If one of the fishermen catches a turbot, I'll buy it, but they seldom get Dover sole off Salcombe. I have to go to Plymouth or Brixham for those.'

It was good to talk to someone who understood the problems. He listened attentively. I told him of my worries that the restaurant was too up-market to be really profitable, but to change it would be to destroy the reputation for excellence that Charles had nurtured, to the detriment of everything else. 'It's bound to lose a lot of its popularity. Some people just won't come anymore, now that Charles is gone. I'm hoping for smaller turnover and more profit, but at the moment, with having to go to the hospital every afternoon and everything else, I know I'm not paying enough attention to that side of the business.'

In answer to a gentle question, I told him how Charles had died. He didn't say much in response, but as we pulled up outside the Galley, just before mid-day, he took my hand and, turning it over, kissed the palm. 'You are a lovely and courageous woman,' he said.

Arrangements were going ahead to auction Hangar, but word was out that it was on the market and it aroused a lot of interest. I had already turned down an offer of £15,000 from one Salcombe resident, and the parents of the baker next door were thinking about buying it for themselves, to be near their grandchildren. One afternoon, when I was working in the restaurant, a call came for me from Hangar, from a man who'd just been shown round with polished expertise by Stephen. He was very excited, he wanted it, desperately.

The solicitor found himself master-minding a contract race, which caused him to become very disgruntled and remark that he had no intention of getting caught up in such proceedings and that he would put a stop to it at once. In the end, the baker's parents got it and the auction was called off. It was probably a bad decision on my part, made because I knew in my heart that I couldn't bear to see Hangar come under the hammer. My solicitor became even more exasperated when I quibbled about paying the agent's fees on the grounds that they had not procured the purchaser.

Completion was set for early May, which meant that the house was still available for Connie to bring her children in the Easter holidays to see their grandfather, for probably the last time. It was a great help to me too, to have her on hand to look after my kids while I coped with the insane circus that Easter always was in the restaurant, and for every business in the town, so great was the year's first influx of visitors.

Easter fell in March in 1975. It had been a mild winter and for the first couple of weeks of the month quite spring-like; but in the week of Good Friday, we got the first snow. Connie's train pulled into Totnes Station in a heavy downfall.

On Thursday, late in the evening, John and I were sitting with the crossword, as had become our habit, when a friend phoned me from the hospital in Plymouth. She had been to Hangar to pick up her son who had been playing with Stephen. The boys had been tumbling around on the floor when Stephen landed awkwardly and dislocated his right thumb. Jean had driven him, with my sister, the twenty-odd miles to the big general hospital in Plymouth. Several unsuccessful attempts had been made to manipulate the thumb back into position and they were now waiting for the night-duty anaesthetist to finish an appendectomy. Then he was coming to anaesthetise Stephen.

I left Judy to lock up and started for Plymouth. The dip switch had still not been fixed, leaving the option of full beam or no lights. I drove all the way, enraging oncoming drivers and expecting any minute to be stopped by the police, but I reached Freedom Fields without mishap.

My evening clothes drew a few curious glances from the usual assortment of people with cut hands and cracked heads who inhabit casualty departments, but the houseman didn't comment.

'I've come straight from work,' I offered in explanation. He probably thought I was some sort of Madam.

Stephen was lying quietly on a trolley, his hand at his side, the thumb joint completely out of true. By this time, it was about one in the morning and it was decided that Connie and Jean had better get back to the other kids. I waited for the anaesthetist, for an hour or more. It was near three before he was brought back to me, groggy and smelling of ether and wet plaster. He had a cast up to his elbow. I made him comfortable on the back seat where he fell into a deep sleep, and braved the snow-covered road home.

I thought it best not to disturb the household at Hangar so I took him back to the Galley. The place was deserted and it was only when I got out to open the door that I remembered I'd given the keys to Judy. Round at the back, the kitchen window of the flat was slightly open and there was a ladder propped where the staircase would eventually be. Hitching up my long skirts, I climbed the ladder and squeezed in through the window, then went down to open the door from the inside.

'Why,' I asked my sleeping son, 'did you have to do this to me on the day before Good Friday?' He was too tall for me to pick up in my arms, so I slung him fireman fashion over my shoulder, carried him up the stairs and tucked him into the bed in my room. I made a bed for myself on the floor beside him.

The weeks that follow Easter normally reverted to winter quiet, especially when the holiday came so early, but we were now open on six nights a week. I moved the children into the flat to ease the problems of finding someone to be with them while I worked. I intended to remain closed on Sunday throughout the season, so that we could have at least one day together. I was also beginning to look forward to Thursdays.

Conversations with John had ranged over most topics. I knew that we agreed about education, but not on who should govern. He loved Sinatra, I loathed him. He was interested in all sport, with the exception of football. I was bored by all team games, particularly football. Not much in common, but tastes that met somewhere in the middle. He stayed on one Thursday night at the beginning of April, after Judy closed the bar and left. He came round the tables with me, helping to pick up the last coffee cups and glasses. He went into the kitchen with a tray. 'He wants to kiss me,' I told myself. 'Well, I'm not going to make it difficult for him.' I didn't move when he came out. His arms went round me and I remember noting as I turned my face up how diffidently they held me. Not the masterful pressure I had expected. The kiss was very satisfactory.

'Will you come out to dinner with me one night?' he asked.

Faintly, a scruple pricked me.

'I'll think about it,' I said.

10

Making a New Start

It was as though Charles had gone out of my life, slamming a great door behind him. I couldn't think about him. Only once, when I was busy packing our belongings ready for the house move, did his image come sharply to my mind. I was pensively discarding most of the contents of the toy cupboard; it seemed that their childhood was being packed away too, when I came across an old briefcase. Among the minutes and agendas of long-past council meetings, was a bag of sticky bullseyes. It floored me. I sank my head in my hands and sobbed for him. If only we could have parted some other way.

May came to help me on moving day, feeling the sadness of leaving as sharply as I did, but we worked hard, without mention of Richard's ashes, and I finally arrived outside the Galley with the last load of clothes, two very annoyed Siamese cats and Lucy the basset-hound crammed into the Golf. It was early afternoon. I just had time to unload under the gaze of the traffic warden, before taking my mother, who was put out because I was half-an-hour late, to the hospital.

There were still a few days to go before legal completion but I was keen to get everyone under the same roof. We had already spent some nights together as a family, even before the flat was ready, sleeping in one room, the children on the available beds and me on a convertible chair borrowed from my mother. I had found it comforting to work at the books by lamplight while they slept; secure in knowing that we were all behind the same closed door.

Most of the furniture had been given away. A few bulky pieces I sold and was surprised to get a good price for some of them. It helped considerably. A couple of months before he died, Charles had bought an old Norton motorbike. When I advertised that for sale I was swamped by calls from enthusiasts and it found itself a new home without trouble.

The ponies were not quite so easy, though Catherine's pony, Bella, being experienced and reliable, sold quite quickly. Milly, the Dartmoor mare, had not been ridden much for the past year, partly because she had had a foal, but also because Lorna was taking her dancing very seriously and the two activities developed muscles differently and were not considered compatible.

Gemma the foal was still unbroken, but she was used to being handled and went to a friend who lived on a farm. That left pretty little Milly. There was no urgency to sell her. She could go on grazing on the adjoining farm owned by Charles' cousin, but I wanted one responsibility less. In one of my Thursday conversations with John, when we remarked on what a coincidence it was that we should both have basset-hounds, I told him about Milly. He thought he might like to buy her for Jonathan and Vicky.

He was a loving, but very strict father. On the one occasion when I saw them all together as a family, the old-fashioned, almost courtly manners of the children made an impression on me. I had called to collect Vicky to take her with Lorna to a ballet class, as her father had asked me. John was at home for the afternoon break between shifts, sprawled wearily in a big armchair. Little Jonathan was pleading with his father to take him out in the boat.

'Not today, darling,' he said, taking the child on to his knee, 'the tide isn't right.'

Pat broke off from the jig-saw puzzle she had spread on a coffee table, to make tea. A pretty, petite blonde, about my own age, her hair worn in a long bob with a fringe. She chatted pleasantly, inviting me to inspect the kitchen improvements John was working on. A certain tension was between them, though they laughed as he told me how he had almost drilled through a power cable. I supposed John was feeling slightly embarrassed because of my presence. Vicky showed no particular liking for the dancing class, but she put a lot of effort into it, hopping from one little plump leg to the other, frowning in concentration. I thought she was adorable.

We met later at Hangar when John came to inspect the pony, both of us in evening clothes ready for our work; for a while, we wandered together round the empty house, feeling its warmth and our growing regard for each other. I had brought Milly in from the field earlier. I didn't have to sell her, he agreed to buy her without really knowing what he was buying, taking my word for it that she could be trusted with the children. He asked me again if I would have dinner with him.

I had thought about it, though not for long and about Pat hardly at all. John had told me she had another man in her life, but that didn't influence me, I would have said yes anyway.

On the way to have dinner in a Queen Anne manor house, deep in the South Hams countryside, we paused. Approaching the bridge at the head of the estuary, John pulled to the side of the road and, taking my hand, led me through a gate, down a path through a graveyard filled with the heavy scent of rhododendrons, to the edge of the high tide. A great moon hung over the wide spread of water, lighting a scene as romantic as any Hollywood musical. I marvelled momentarily, that he, a newcomer, should have found this place, but standing close to him, fitting so snugly into his embrace, I didn't dwell on it.

There would be no turning back after this. I had not thought beyond the immediate, stolen pleasure of being with him. It was clear that I must become his mistress soon, but it didn't occur to me that he planned anything more. Philandering men rarely actually leave their wives and I did not want or hope for that.

Once the sale of Hangar was completed, I knew a brief period of happiness such as I have never experienced, before or since. My solicitor had signed his way through a couple of fat cheque books and all creditors had been paid. There was even a little money left over. Freedom, and money in the bank! It was heady stuff.

At six in the evening, sitting at my dressing-table getting ready to go downstairs at seven, I'd hear the restaurant staff arriving. The chefs had been at work since about three. Bar shutters were raised and music would burst from the music centre. Charles Aznavour was popular that year; 'Dance in the Old Fashioned Way' and snatches of another lyric, 'Die of love', drifted up and cheered me. Later, I would be able to get away, and John and I could spend half an hour sitting in the car in a quiet lane above North Sands.

One night, anticipation must have shown in my face. My friend from the dress shop had been in for a meal, and she said to me as I handed her her coat, 'Eunice, you look so happy. You really do.' She said it in a conspiratorial undertone, as she might have said, 'Eunice, your slip is showing.'

The finished flat above the restaurant was delightful. Now that the extension to the bakery below was complete, we had access to its flat roof from the French doors in the living-room and from there to our own flat roof, giving us a huge balcony with views as fine as any in the world.

Another bonus for me was that I seldom had to cook, except when we were closed on Sundays. Staff and family had to eat whatever the chef wanted to get rid of, so we tended to get plenty of chicken and duck in our diet. After a while, this brought pleas of 'Couldn't we please have sausage and beans?' Once, when gleanies or guinea fowl were on the menu, Stephen had a friend to supper. His mother told me, when she came into the bar a few days later, that her son had reported being given guinea pig and chips.

The children seemed to adjust well. Stephen developed an interest in ferreting and tended to go back to the fields around Hangar much of the time. I wouldn't let him keep a polecat ferret in a hutch on the roof. The animals we had were enough of a problem, so it was kept in a friend's backyard. Lorna was pleased that she could now come home from school for lunch and she soon struck up a friendship with the baker's daughters. Catherine worried me. I was unhappy about some of her new friendships and the loving rapport we used to have had gone, temporarily, I hoped. I thought sometimes that she was angry with me for not being the one that died. Fourteen is a particularly bad age at which to lose a parent. I planned to take them all on holiday at the end of the season.

Her fifteenth birthday cards were still on display when John came up to the flat for the first time, after closing on a Thursday night at the end of April. I carried up a tray of coffee. We stood out on the roof for a while, winding down after the bustle of the evening, listening to the tinkling music of a thousand halyards slapping against their aluminium masts in the stiff breeze. Inside, in the warmth and glow of lamplight, we drank our coffee then, closing the fire door quietly between us and the sleeping children, we went to bed together in my tiny room.

My fortieth birthday, two weeks later, was my happiest. Judy and the waitresses gave me a present of perfume and a customer of long standing unexpectedly produced a beautiful crucifix – 'To protect you'. John privately handed me a heavy gold locket. He had suggested a gold waist chain to wear secretly, under my clothes. It was a romantic notion, but one that I didn't care for.

I had been invited to the May Ball at Dartmouth Royal Naval College and had been looking forward to going, but John was upset by the idea and since I had been feeling lately that I had stepped on to a merry-go-round that was moving a little too fast for comfort, in order to slow it down a bit, I eventually wrote begging to be excused.

Catherine came in from the beach one Sunday afternoon, saying she had lost Lucy on the other side of the estuary. The dog had always been neurotic, the runt of the litter, chosen from the kennels by Catherine because she was afraid she was doomed to be a brood bitch. Strangers couldn't get near her and her eyesight wasn't too good either. Being a hound, she relied on her sense of smell. Once she became separated, she would run away, even from people she knew.

I was upset. She was Catherine's dog, but had attached herself to me. She was my shadow, always just behind me. When she was spayed, I could hardly move from my chair for fear she would burst her wound, because every time I got up, she dragged herself from her basket to follow me. A pack animal, she would never have the gumption to board the ferry and find her way home, or, like Lassie, trot round the edge.

We went back to the beach to search for her, but it was no use. I asked people on both sides of the water to let me know if they saw her, but there was nothing more I could do. Several times I got calls to say she was wandering about in the fields at Portlemouth, but by the time I got across on the ferry, she had vanished. At least I knew she was still in the area.

Late one night, hours after the ferry had stopped running, a caller rang to say she was on the ferry slipway. John was in the bar and immediately volunteered to take me over in his boat. He must just slip home to get the keys. When he came back, Pat was with him, full of concern for the dog. The three of us set out together, but getting out to the boat and freeing it from its mooring was such a lengthy business, by the time we nosed on to the ferry hard, Lucy had gone again.

Spring Bank Holiday was approaching. It was never the major event that Easter was, but it still required special preparation for the upsurge in the number of visitors. Connie had come down again from Aberdeen. My father was sinking and my mother now hardly left his side.

He lay with his eyes closed, not moving, but we knew he was aware of our presence. He smiled slightly when we whispered to him, 'Connie's here.'

Then he spoke, very softly. 'What should I do?' he asked, 'Should I hold on, or should I let go now?'

A most terrible question. We, his children, had agreed that to prolong his life chemically would be cruel and had told the hospital staff of our feelings. Why it was me that answered, I don't know, but I stroked his thin brown hand and said, 'We think you should let go now, darling.'

That night, after the last customer was seated, I went to meet John. We sat in my car in the lane and I told him what my father had said. He found it hard to believe. We sat in silence for some time before he asked, 'Do you think, if you have something very unpleasant to do, that you should get it over with quickly?'

'What do you mean?'

'I'm going to tell Pat how I feel about you.'

At that moment I didn't much care, but in principle, if he was determined to do it, it was better done sooner than later.

Father died the next morning at about 7.30, on Wednesday, 22 May. Mother had been beside him all night. I was glad my brother and sister were on hand to sustain her and help with organising the funeral. The restaurant was too busy for me to take time off.

I went to work as usual the night of his death and was kept scuttling about so that I had no time to think of sorrow until at the end of the evening, when I was invited to join an elderly local couple at their table, for a drink. They were having their splendid house renovated. The wife was telling me the usual sorry tale of disappearing plumbers and builders who didn't turn up till noon, when she started to weep, probably the effect of an excess of gin. 'It's absolutely awful,' she wailed, 'I've ordered gold-plated dolphin taps for the bathroom, and they can't deliver them for six weeks.'

We had to have Father buried on Friday, because of the bank holiday. It was distressing for Lil. In the Irish Catholic culture in which she grew up, it was the custom to hold a wake week, when the body could be viewed by friends who would drop in for food and drink and to recall times spent with the deceased. She had the coffin at home for only one day, before we four members of his immediate family and a couple of friends sat in the echoing church at Malborough to hear his burial service. For the second time in four months, we stood by an open grave in the cemetery at the top of the hill, five paces from Charles' on the other side of the path.

Saturday was hot and the town filled up fast. I had the usual phone call from John at 7.30 in the morning when he went on duty and expected no more contact with him that day. The Marine, too, was busy.

Service that night went fairly smoothly, despite the number and size of the parties eating. I had borrowed extra chairs from the Masonic Hall and squeezed two extra places on to each table. People enjoyed being squashed, I'd realised, it seemed to convince them that they must be in the right place. Certainly they were a tolerant, good-humoured crowd that night.

Around 11.30, the last diners had been called to their table. I went to stand by the front door. Some kind of sentry was necessary on such a night, to keep out those who wanted to go on drinking after the pubs turned them out. I propped the door open, to try to blow some fresh air into the crush in the bar, glad of the chance to cool off myself.

I was surprised to see John. Not his usual debonair self. He looked down at me earnestly.

'Can you get away for five minutes?'

I glanced over my shoulder at the hubbub behind me.

'Not just yet.'

'There's something I want to talk to you about.'

It amounted to dereliction of duty, but this was clearly important. I went to find Judy who had been managing the floor with me and asked her to hold the fort for a few minutes.

We threaded our way up Fore Street, through the revellers, to the peace of Cliff House Gardens, a small green enclosure surrounding the war memorial. We sat on a bench at the water's edge. Once again, as if ordered by some celestial film director, a magical moon shone centre stage.

'Pat is talking about leaving me,' he began.

'Because of me?'

Hard to understand why else she would want to leave this charming man.

'No, she's still got this boyfriend she was seeing while I was away. If she goes,' he went on, 'will you have the children to live with you?'

The question stunned me. I knew my answer instantly, but had to grope for the right words to explain: 'John, I've been a widow for four months. I've got a business to run. I hardly have time to see my own three kids. I just can't take on two more, younger children.'

He didn't argue, or turn sour at my refusal; he just quietly smoked a cigarette, then stood up and we climbed the path back to the road.

Walking back to the Galley, I struggled with tears. I felt guilty, hating to refuse him anything, but I didn't believe Pat would abandon her children. I had seen her with them, she plainly loved them. It was unthinkable.

I glanced up at him. He was obviously worried, but in this, I couldn't help him. I needed what little was left of my spiritual strength to keep the lid on my grief for my father, so that I wouldn't depress my customers.

11

John Allen Gains His Freedom

With bank holiday Saturday safely behind, it was possible to relax just a bit. On Sunday and Monday, business was still brisk but less frantic; there would be no more mad surges until the start of the school holidays, by which time the traders were conditioned and fit for the contest.

There was no early morning call from John on Tuesday morning. I was upstairs, sorting out the weekend takings, ready for the daily trip to the bank, when the door opened and he came in, Vicky and Jonathan following apprehensively, close behind. He looked handsome in an immaculate, pale grey suit with a pink shirt.

He came only a step into the room and stood drawing deeply on a cigarette, the children peering out from behind his legs. He said flatly: 'Pat's gone.'

The hand that took the cigarette back to his mouth was shaking, but he was otherwise perfectly in control. As his cuff slipped back, I saw that there were deep scratches running down his forearm.

'What happened?'

'We had a row first thing this morning. She's packed and gone off to meet her boyfriend. She's taken her car.'

This was awful. I hadn't bargained for this, but it was not something we could continue to discuss in front of the children.

'I've got to go to work now,' he continued. 'Can I leave

the kids with you? I'm sorry to ask, but I didn't know what else to do.'

'Oh, yes. Of course they can stay here.'

'I'll get something sorted out.'

'That's OK.'

He bent down to Jonathan: 'I want you to stay here with Mrs Yabsley, until I get back from work. I'll be back at lunchtime. Be a good boy and take care of Vicky.' He plonked a kiss on each head. They looked back at him, round-eyed, but didn't protest when he turned and went back down the stairs.

I led them through to the living-room, thinking to set them up with some painting or drawing, but Catherine stepped into her big-sister role and took them off to see the boats at Batson Creek. Little Vicky didn't say much and Jonathan, exquisitely polite, prefaced every remark with 'Excuse me'. I wasn't certain if they had seen the row or understood what was going on. They didn't mention their mother.

John came back about three, suggesting we go to the beach. He'd been back to the flat to change into lighter clothes and to collect the children's swimming things. I fell in with the idea, glad to get away to where we could talk freely. We put the kids, his two and my Lorna, into the back of my car and drove to Thurlestone, a neighbouring coastal village.

We sat on a rug, watching the children play in the sand. He was calm. He told me things had been difficult between him and Pat for some time. She had met another man while he was away for such a long time, in hospital. When he came home, they'd agreed to try to make the marriage work, but had been finding the going hard.

'How did you get those scratches on your arm?'

'I told her I wanted to finish it. She flew at me. I put my arms up to protect my face.'

He'd had time to think a bit about how he was going to cope.

'I'll have to see about getting an au pair to live in. I've swapped a shift tonight and the girl next door will probably baby-sit for me tomorrow.'

I had to be back in time to open. We called the children. As I dried Jonathan's wiry little body and helped him into his clothes, I couldn't believe that his mother would leave him. She would come back, for sure, when she'd had time to cool off. I dropped them at their gate.

'Will I see you later?' he asked. I nodded.

'I'll come up, when things get quiet.'

I escaped at about 10.30. He poured wine for us. 'I rang my mother,' he said. 'She's going to come down tomorrow, to take care of the kids for a while. Can I borrow your car, to pick her up from Totnes?'

No problem. I fetched the keys from my jacket pocket.

A thin wail from an upstairs room interrupted us. John went up and reappeared a moment later, carrying a flushed and tearful Vicky.

'She's got earache,' he said. He sat, rocking her on his knee, but she would not be comforted.

'I'll go and find those special drops,' he said to her. He passed her over to me and went to the bathroom, coming back with a battered biscuit tin. He rummaged through until he found what he was looking for. 'She often gets this trouble,' he added.

I held her in my lap, talking gently, trying to soothe her, while he put in the drops. He took her back in his arms and after a while, when she became quiet, he carried her back upstairs to bed. At about eleven, I rose to go. I couldn't stay out too long, or my own children would be left alone. At the top of the steps that led down to the children's playground and my shortest path home, I turned to look back at the house. He was standing in the lighted window, watching me go. We each raised a hand in farewell and I went on, down the steps. I had not seen Jonathan.

I did not see John at all the next day, I am sure of that. On the next, Thursday, he came to my flat in the morning, to return my car keys. He was light-hearted, relaxed, sprawling in the armchair, drinking coffee. He and his mother had decided it would be best if she took the children back with her to Bournemouth until he could make a better arrangement.

Connie turned up. If she was surprised to see a man in my flat, she hid it. They got on well immediately and John suggested that as we were all free for the day, that we go to Dartmouth for lunch.

We took the coastal route, past Slapton Ley. At Strete, we stopped to lean on a gate and look out over the meadows to the chain of cliffs and beaches stretching away towards Berry Head. I must have shivered in the chill wind. John took off his jacket and put it round my shoulders, as though I were a fragile, Victorian maiden, removing any doubt my sister might still have had about the nature of our relationship.

After lunch we went, at the invitation of a man we met in the restaurant, to watch a cricket match at the Royal Naval College. For three troubled people, two newly bereaved and one just parted from his children, we found plenty to laugh at that day. Shaggy-dog stories carefully timed and delivered by John, even the names above a Dartmouth estate agent's – Letcher and Scorer – seemed hilariously funny. I reflected on the way home that it must have been the release from the terrible tensions of the past few days that made us all slightly hysterical.

June brought a little peace. Connie went back to Aberdeen and John's visits became more frequent, though I resisted the pressure he was beginning to put on me, to let him move in with me. Arguments that it would have a detrimental effect on the children, that it would shock people, that it was just too soon, had no effect on him. Only when I pointed out that it could cause business to drop off, did he pay attention.

'That's the first thing you've said to convince me,' he said. 'OK, I'll wait three weeks.' I laughed at his impetuosity.

'Three weeks won't be enough.'

'Well don't ask me to go away and come back in three

years when I'm divorced.'

On most afternoons I spent an hour or two in his flat, which remained tidy, but began to look dirty and neglected. He hadn't heard from Pat, but said that Vicky and Jonathan had settled in well with an aunt; apparently he intended to leave them there, at least for the time being.

He began to make overtures of friendship towards my children. Catherine was difficult to approach by either of us, but he bought Lorna a watch and took her on a trip, with me, to see Kitley Caves. Apart from a startled 'double take', when she saw him take my hand, she appeared unconcerned by his arrival on the scene.

A fishing trip with Stephen, who still had his right arm in plaster because of his repeatedly dislocating thumb, aborted abruptly when John fell overboard, not from his boat, but from the dinghy. He had rowed out to his mooring which, unfortunately, was just in front of the Marine Hotel dining-room, in the little dinghy, overburdened with his own thirteen-stone frame, Stephen, various bags of tackle and food, and Fleur, the basset-hound.

Coming alongside the boat, he had tried to persuade Fleur to leap aboard, but she wasn't keen. Seizing her by the scruff of the neck, he stood up and tried to lift her into the tiny cockpit, but she resisted and, stretching her crooked little legs to their full nine inches, pushed against the side, forcing boat and dinghy to swing away from each other. John had no choice but to drop the hound in the water and to swiftly follow her.

It was lunchtime and the spectacle was enjoyed by the diners at the Marine, most of whom he would have to face that evening. His watch was ruined too. Fleur was rescued, Stephen remained dry and, I'm afraid, unimpressed by the display of boatmanship.

I was still getting reports of sightings of my own dog, who had been lost for four or five weeks by now. I was amazed to hear that she was still surviving, then I got some heartening news. The couple who owned one of the beautiful houses on the water's edge, on the Portlemouth side of the estuary, rang to tell me that she had been coming regularly to their back gate at about midnight. They had been leaving food out for her and had watched from a window while she ate it. Any movement from the house sent her running for cover. On my next trip for supplies, I bought a crate of tinned dog food and delivered it to the house.

John devised a way to catch her. The path from the back gate to the house sloped downhill. If a string were attached to the gate and the bowl of food placed so that as the dog ate, it slid steadily down the slope, a person lying hidden might wait until she had ventured far enough down the path to pull the gate closed behind her. She would be trapped. Basset-hounds are not great at jumping fences.

It was worth a try. We got the agreement of the house owners and every night that the tide was favourable, at the end of service, John waited for me in the boat at one of the town's landing jetties and took me across to the other side.

Padding in our boat shoes between the high banks of the lane that leads from the ferry landing to the house, we were like saboteurs. We spoke only in whispers, for fear the dog would hear us, but we wrapped our arms tightly round each other, revelling in being away from inquisitive eyes. Almost sick from lack of sleep, we kept watch. From our vantage point on a low garden wall, we could see up the road and across the water to the lights of Salcombe. Several times we almost had her. Once, John's arm across my shoulder tightened.

'She's coming,' he said, close to my ear. She appeared wraith-like out of the gloom and cautiously approached the bowl of food, worried that it was just inside the gateway. Every few seconds she raised her head like a gazelle and sniffed the air. We heard the bowl slither a little way down the path. John waited until she was almost inside then, fearing she would finish the food and bolt, he pulled the string to close the gate behind her. No use. She did a supple U-turn, squeezed through the narrowing gap and headed back the way she came, long ears flapping.

Another time we met her in the lane, coming towards us as we made our way to the house. I got within five feet of her. She stopped in her tracks. I crouched and called softly to her, convinced that she would recognise my voice and come to me: 'Lucy, come on, dear little girl, Lucy.'

She didn't know me. She turned and ran towards the open fields.

I decided to spend the money I got from the sale of the Norton on a new watch for John's birthday. I went to a good jeweller in Torquay and bought the best the money would buy. A thin, elegant gold case, brown face and brown leather strap. Waterproof.

I gave it to him at five o'clock on the morning of his birthday, as he rose from my narrow bed, to leave before anyone discovered him there. It was examined by the light of my bedside lamp and pronounced beautiful. He strapped it to his wrist, kissed me and slipped out, down the stairs and into the street. I heard the front door click and his footsteps recede. Hard to tell if he really thought it beautiful, his own taste was a little less restrained.

His appreciation of my gift was put to the test a week or so later. We had spent our afternoon's leisure cruising round the harbour and were savouring the last half hour before coming ashore to start work, sipping wine, riding at anchor in the warm sun. On a tape, Kiri te Kanawa sang 'Songs from the Auvergne'. John was lolling, glass in hand, with his elbow resting on the gunwale. I faced him, dreamily enjoying the gentle motion and soothing slap of water on the hull, when I saw the buckle fastening on his watch strap give way slightly. A small movement of his wrist and, as though it had been deliberately loosened and before I could warn him, the watch dropped over the side, into about twelve feet of water, with the tide rising.

We were both aghast, peering in disbelief into the depths. Thoughts that flashed through my mind of hiring a skin diver to retrieve it were quickly discarded. There were no means of marking the spot and it would almost certainly sink in the mud after a couple of minutes. I found my voice: 'Ah well, never mind.'

'We can't just write it off.'

'I think we're going to have to.'

'Let's make a note of our position, then perhaps we can get someone to come out with a metal detector at low tide.'

'I think we must be in the deep-water channel.'

The boat was swinging slowly to and fro on the anchor line, light and shadow playing on the dancing surface of the water, when suddenly, it came into view from underneath her. We both spotted it at once, glinting on the sandy bottom.

'There it is,' John exclaimed. 'I wonder if I could get it.'

I thought not, it was down too deep. 'Please don't worry about it. It doesn't matter.'

'It's nice of you to say it doesn't matter, but I'm going to try to get it back.'

He took off his shirt and trousers and dived over the side in his underpants. Twice he failed; each time he came up for air, I begged him to give up. It was hard to keep track of the watch with the movement of the boat, but on the third attempt he came up triumphant. For a week after, he complained that he couldn't get the distinctive smell of estuary mud out of his nostrils.

Our affair had hardly begun before it caused comment. Most people were too polite to say anything direct, but our movements became the subject of more than usual interest. If John and I slipped away to my flat, late in the evening, to do nothing more scandalous than watch the news, some member of staff would find an urgent reason to break in on us, to consult. My mother expressed her disquiet, but I could not see that she need be concerned. I was, after all, a free woman.

A neighbour, perching prettily on a bar stool one night, took it upon herself to warn me against John. She'd heard that he was not to be trusted. She couldn't say on what the information was based. Another young woman, who had been instrumental in getting me invited to the ball at the Naval College, repeated a remark she claimed was made by my disappointed escort, that it was such a pity that a woman like me should have the misfortune to cross the path of a man like John.

It was puzzling. John was tall, physically commanding, reasonably handsome, affable and charming. A consort to please any woman. Such venom must be rooted in jealousy. I kept some of these things to myself, not wanting to hurt John but I told him what my neighbour had said. He shrugged it off. She couldn't possibly have known anything discreditable about him. No one knew him around here. It was just malicious gossip. I decided he was right and dismissed the comments, but they slightly marred my peace of mind as did another small incident.

I came downstairs one morning to find the boy who had put the torch to the Galley, leaning on the hatch, chatting casually to the chef. He'd been released from Borstal and now felt free to revisit his old haunts. I ordered him out at once and left him and the chef in no doubt that he was a barred person. He didn't argue about going, but took his time to leave, sauntering to the door, bestowing on me as he passed, a look of sneering contempt.

One constantly nagging worry was about to be removed. I got a telephone call to tell me that Lucy had been caught. The young man who worked in the garden on the other side of the road from the house where we had been trying to corner her, had managed to trap her. He had been scything long grass in a paddock next to the house, when he'd come upon her curled up asleep. She'd made a nest for herself, where she spent her days resting, going out at night to forage for food. Never a speedy animal, he managed to grab her by the tail before she woke up. He got a grip on her and carried her to his employer's house where they shut her in a small downstairs room before phoning me.

The risk of losing her again if I tried to bring her back on the ferry was great and I was not sure what condition she would be in after nine weeks living on her limited wits, so I decided to collect her in the car. John drove me the nine road miles round to the house, less than a mile away as the seagull flies, where we were shown into a back kitchen.

She slunk out of her prison, tail between her legs. The colour had faded from her coat, the tawny patches were dull, and she was extremely thin, but she was otherwise fine. I slipped a collar round her neck and clipped on the leash. Crouching beside her, I stroked and petted her, but she didn't respond. Going home, she cowered on the back seat, looking as wretchedly miserable as only a basset-hound can. She still didn't know me.

Once home, she accepted food and milk and suffered me to give her a warm bath. She was lying on the old sofa, drying off on a towel, when realisation began to dawn. She got down, clamped her nose to the floor and began coursing from room to room, steadily increasing speed until she was running. She leapt first on one bed then on another, giving excited little yelps, then rushed madly back to jump on the sofa and off again. Back again to roll on the children's beds then to where I sat watching her antics, to cover me with licks and kisses, quite beside herself with joy.

12

Rumours and Revelations

I have to admit that I did not think much about Jonathan and Vicky. My life was full and busy and when images of them living with an elderly aunt intruded, I either reassured myself that their mother would surely be in contact, or I shut them from my mind, in much the same way as I deal with issues like the slaughter of elephants, choosing not to give myself pain by dwelling on things I cannot change.

Whether John contributed to their upkeep, I didn't inquire. Beyond an occasional anecdote about funny things the children had said, he mentioned them no more often than the two boys by his first marriage, which was rarely. He sometimes told the story of when Pat and the children had been to a children's Christmas party at a hotel where he was working. He was playing Father Christmas and, after making his entrance in costume and giving each child a present, including his own, he left the room and reappeared a little later in his managerial pinstripes. Jonathan had rushed up to him: 'Daddy where were you? You just missed Father Christmas. He was here a minute ago!'

Pat didn't get in touch and left no word about where she intended to go. She had left some belongings behind, clothing of her own and the children's, and jewellery, two long, heavy gold chains, very fashionable at the time, a St Christopher and several rings. John gave some clothing to families in the town, the jewellery he offered to me.

I thought him a bit insensitive. He might have known that I would refuse it, not caring to wear another woman's finery, most of it probably given by him; but men are pragmatists. Perhaps he couldn't see the difference between taking her jewels and taking her husband, but husbands and wives are not personal possessions, however long a marriage may last. I suggested he sell them. I knew the second-hand jeweller Percy Diamond was in town and went to the Salcombe Hotel to find him.

In his youth, Percy must have been impressive, rivalling Prince Monolulu on the race-courses of England for dramatic effect. His appearance was still striking, but his tall figure had grown spindly with age. The loud check suit, repository for dozens of small gold trinkets, sagged round his shoulders and backside.

He came to my flat for tea and we showed him what was on offer. In other circumstances, they were things I would be pleased to own, but I was glad when Percy agreed to buy it all, except for a garnet ring, the St Christopher and a few pieces of costume jewellery of no particular value. Those I wrapped and locked in the safe.

Disposing of the clothes and the deal with Percy cleared some of the debris left by Pat's abrupt departure. It was not possible for John, nor did he try, to eliminate from their home all reminders of his family. A framed photograph of the children in the uniform of a private school, taken before they came to Salcombe, hung on the sitting-room wall. In the bedroom, the very feminine dressing-table stood in the window; the lamp John had wired for her, to hang just above her head when seated, remained poised to light the mirror, reflecting now a dusty surface devoid of perfume and make-up. He had done no more work on the breakfast bar.

It seemed unlikely that the hotel management would allow him to go on living in such a large flat alone. I knew the family who owned the hotel; the father not so much as a personal friend, but I'd met him several times at social gatherings and in the course of council work. His daughter and her husband had been on closer terms when Charles was alive. I thought they would probably suggest moving John into staff quarters inside the hotel, but if that was their plan, it went wrong.

He startled me by turning up in the middle of a fairly busy evening. I was upstairs at my desk, probably finding a bill for a customer, when I looked up and saw him standing in the doorway, dressed in slacks and sweater, his dinner suit and shirt draped over his arm. He gave me a minute to absorb the shock before he spoke: 'I've been sacked.'

It was quietly spoken. Head bent, he watched for my reaction from under lowered brows, a wary, questioning look that I was to come to know well. I sat unmoved, mulling over this new disaster. My reactions are slow and deliberate, he had yet to learn that.

'I was given an ultimatum,' he said. 'Give you up, or lose my job.'

'That's ridiculous. What does it have to do with them?'

'They can't have their restaurant manager carrying on an affair with the owner of a rival establishment. Conflict of loyalties.'

A plausible reason, but I was angry, insulted. What right had they to even comment on my personal life?

'I'm sorry,' he said, 'what else could I do? I told them to keep the job. I can't give you up.'

'Don't you have to work out your notice?'

'Probably, but I just walked out.'

I wondered briefly how they were coping with the crisis in the hotel dining-room and felt slightly better.

'I've got to get out of the flat.'

'When?'

'They want me out by Friday.'

'That only gives us three days!'

'I know. I'm sorry,' he repeated.

'You'll have to come here.'

'I've got nowhere else to go.'

Having just got my home arranged to my satisfaction, I now had to find room for his belongings. The only item of furniture was a bookcase, which I didn't particularly like, the rest was clothes, papers, books, photographs, ornaments, all the effects gathered over a lifetime and not amounting to much, when seen in a heap. They still overcrowded my flat, spoiling my pleasure in it. The washing-machine and dryer were a boon.

I helped him with the move. I took the new school trunk I'd bought ready for Stephen's departure to boarding school in September up to Powderham Villa to carry odds and ends we would otherwise have had to pack into boxes. By Friday, he was installed. Catherine came home for the weekend to find him there. There had been no time to prepare her.

There was no point in continuing the pretence that we were not sleeping together. To begin with, I put a bed for him in the shower room, the only available space, but it was clear that the internal partitions above the Galley would have to be rearranged, getting rid of a dining-room and my tiny room to make us a double bedroom. On a trip to Plymouth to buy wallpaper and lampshades, John saw a lace-trimmed four-poster bed in a department store.

'I can see you in that bed,' he said.

'Don't be silly, we can get something for half that price.'

'No. You should sleep in a bed like that.'

He signed a cheque and organised delivery.

'You are,' I said to him, not for the first time, 'just too good to be true.'

'That's the last of my money,' he said. 'Still, I expect you'll feed me.'

He earned his board and lodging several times over. At first, he helped in the bar, the rate at which we worked coming as something of a shock to him. Not the sedate pace of a four-star hotel. Gradually, he took over more of the running and the hard graft of the place, until we were working in tandem. At his insistence, we gave up closing on Sunday.

Stephen and Lorna were either too young or too reticent to express the bewilderment and resentment they probably felt at the sudden imposition of a substitute father. Not so Catherine. She tackled me on the subject, her little face screwed up in mutinous anger.

'What's he doing here?' she demanded.

No explanation I could give was adequate. I told her I knew he could never replace her father, but that in time I hoped we could all be happy together. She was unconvinced. I ended with a feeble attempt at making her understand how I felt about him.

'Well, I don't trust him.' She spat it at me.

I considered telling him he must go; to stay with his mother, anywhere, but rejected the idea. I loved this man. I would do anything in the world for my kids, but not that. I wanted him and in this if nothing else, I intended to put my own desires first. There was nothing I could do but wait and pray for my child to be reconciled.

Not long after that, the chef gave notice. I was never given the reason, he chose to tell John rather than me. He came upstairs to where I sat getting ready for the evening, to break the news, his face full of consternation.

'When is he going?' I asked.

'He's given a fortnight's notice.'

'Well, we're lucky. It gives us a bit of time. Don't worry, it's a blow, but we'll get round it.'

Judy provided the answer. She knew of a young chef keen to change his job. I knew him too, had in fact known him since he was at school. I used to refuse to serve him in the bar when he was under age. Now he was the father of a family living locally. I rang him.

I continued to reward my solicitor's efforts to help me by being stubborn and difficult, a situation not of my choosing, and one I regretted. I would have preferred his approval. My

frequent visits to his office as co-trustee became occasions to
dread. Not that he treated me with less than perfect consideration; it was just that somehow, he always managed to rob
me of hope, a knack probably acquired through long years of
counselling criminals.

Driving into Kingsbridge on the way to answer a summons
from his secretary, I warned John that he had better be
careful how he spoke to me for the rest of the day: 'I am
about to become very depressed.' He arranged to wait for me
in the café where we always had coffee and did a crossword
after finishing our chores in Kingsbridge. One of the things I
loved about him so much was that he took pleasure in such
things. The office or, more properly, chamber, at the top of a
wide flight of stairs, might have been constructed as a stage
set: an expanse of carpet between the door and a massive
desk, walls lined with shelves, crammed with mainly red-
bound books, windows set high up, shedding dusty light on
the smooth dark head of the leading character. I took the
client's chair and, facing him across the glassy surface of his
desk, waited to hear why he had sent for me.

The subject of the interview turned out to be John and his
occupation of the Galley, an almost insufferable intrusion
into my private affairs, but I tolerated the questions because
no doubt he felt he had an unpleasant duty to ask them. How
much better it would have been for both of us, if Charles had
never made a will. My answers were civil, if not full.

'You have,' he said, 'every right to be in love with him.'

'Thank you.'

'Did you know that he is an undischarged bankrupt with a
criminal record?'

Thank God for my slow reactions. The information
dropped through all my levels of consciousness like lead
down a shot tower.

'No. I didn't know that.'

I tried to keep my voice even and steady, searching for a
way to end the conversation so that I could get out without

breaking down. Out in the teeming street, making my way up the hill, the few yards to the café where John waited, I looked straight ahead, fearing to meet a friend and have to exchange pleasantries. He got up when he saw me and went to the counter to fetch coffee for me.

'Bad, was it?' he asked, setting it in front of me.

'Pretty bloody. He told me you are an undischarged bankrupt with a criminal record.'

I watched him. Hardly a muscle moved in his face but his expression changed from genial to tense apprehension.

'Is it true?' I persisted.

'Let's go somewhere else. I can't talk to you here.'

In the car, the tears started: 'I don't believe this is happening to me.' I remembered numerous newspaper reports I'd read, of court cases where silly widows had parted with their money because a plausible conman had feigned love for them; the judges' scathing comments about gullible women. At Malborough, he turned right, away from Salcombe.

'Where are we going?'

'I can't take you home like this. We'll go to Soar Mill Cove, it'll be quiet there.'

We parked at the head of the narrow green valley. He took his pristine handkerchief and began mopping my cheeks, as though I were a four-year-old.

'I suppose now, you don't believe I love you.'

'No, I don't believe it.'

'I've been on the verge of telling you so many times. You kept on saying, "You're too good to be true," and it got harder and harder. I was so afraid of losing you.'

'Maybe it's the Galley you're afraid of losing.'

'I'd like to know what put that idea in your head. I could understand it if you owned the Mirabelle. The Galley's nice, but you don't even own it.'

'True, but it's a means of earning a living.'

'There are easier ways to earn a living than working sixteen hours a day in someone else's restaurant.'

That couldn't be denied either.

Explanations, when they came, were brief. In the early seventies, when he and Pat had been living in the Manchester area, Post Office workers began a protracted strike. John had set up a freelance mail-delivery service. It was very successful, gaining strength and expanding, when suddenly, the strike was called off and his services were no longer required. He was left with three sacks of undelivered mail.

'Honestly,' he said, 'they were only circulars and that sort of thing. I checked. Junk mail, so I took it out to a corner of a car park and burnt it. Someone saw me and reported me to the police. I was arrested for tampering with Her Majesty's mail.'

'What an idiot.'

'Perhaps, but my solicitor was convinced I would get off with a fine or a suspended sentence. He couldn't believe it when the judge gave me three years. Neither could I. He said I might have been burning old ladies' pension books. I had a mortgage on the house, which I couldn't repay. That's when they made me bankrupt.'

'So you were in prison, not hospital?'

'I'm sorry, yes, but it's the easiest way to explain a long absence from home.'

'No kidney problems?'

'No.'

'And Pat waited for you?'

'Yes. It was very hard on her, with the kids so young. I started my sentence in Winson Green. It was terrible, I can't tell you, but after a while they shifted me to an open prison. I thought, if I've got to do this, I can bear to do it here, but I got remission and I was released after a year.'

Sitting beside him, gradually becoming more composed, I heard him out and made my own judgement. I had been right. He was too good to be true. The wit, charm and intelligence were all there, all genuine, but flawed by an under lying inability to face the truth. He was clever, but weak and stupid too.

'You aren't going to tell me I've got to get out of your life, are you?' he begged. 'I've paid for what I did.'

'What you did was ridiculous.'

'I know, I could have just reposted the lot, in batches, but I didn't hurt anybody, only myself.'

'And Pat.'

'I do love you, and if you let me stay, I promise you won't regret it. I want to take care of you.'

I'd heard that before.

'OK. I won't send you packing.'

13

Inquisition

Bankrupts are not allowed to hold bank accounts. I made John close his and did what little else could be done to mend matters. The solicitor agreed to see him after I pleaded that he might be reassured to meet an obviously decent man who had paid the price for an act of folly.

This time, I waited in the café for John to return from the high chamber.

'Well,' I asked when he joined me, 'what did he say?'

'He said you were the last, the very last, person anyone would have expected to behave in the way you have.'

'Really? You mean taking a live-in lover without waiting a proper interval after my husband's death?'

'Yeah, and a married man at that.'

'Funny, he's one of the few people I would have expected to understand.'

We settled again into a harmonious routine of living and working together, but the shine had gone and my efforts to weld us into a family group were failing. Nothing I did or said could soothe Catherine's wounded feelings and she continued to be bitterly hostile. When she learned that Stephen was to go to boarding school in the autumn, she said, 'The poor thing!' She looked daggers at me. 'It's such a shame about you.' Plainly she thought it was a move on my part to be rid of another of my children.

It was unjust. I would have liked him to stay at the local

school, but it was failing him, or from the head's point of view, he was failing to fit in. My fears that he was underachieving were dismissed as an over-reaction. Most teachers, in common with most doctors, know that mothers cannot look at their children objectively.

I discovered by accident that he had been playing truant. My mother bumped into him wandering about Kingsbridge one day. He had been attending for registration, pursuing his own pleasures all day, then rejoining a class in the late afternoon to catch the school bus home. It was easy for him to do. The school was split over three sites around the town, with pupils moving between each at changes of period. In four months of perpetual truancy, none of the staff ever realised he was missing.

Work in the restaurant was going to prevent me from giving my son much more than minimal supervision, just as he was entering adolescence. This consideration convinced me that I must find the money to send him to a school where they would at least notice his presence or absence and might even appreciate the qualities of his bright and original mind.

I wrote to a retired naval officer living locally, who I knew was governor of a school on the edge of Dartmoor. He arranged for Stephen to be interviewed by the head. Having not taken the Common Entrance examination, he would have to be judged on his personality.

John was supportive, and drove me and a rebellious Stephen to the meeting. He waited in the car while we were shown round the school.

'Nobody fails here,' said the head to Stephen. 'We have produced admirals and archbishops.'

'All I want,' said my son, in a determined effort to scupper his own chances, 'is to be a chippy.'

That more or less clinched it. He was in. I spent my spare moments in the following weeks making the necessary preparations. Buying uniform, equipment, a tuck box and the brass-bound trunk.

At the end of the season we took a short break, visiting my sister in Scotland, returning to a town settled into winter hibernation, which I loved and John found tedious. We opened the Galley at weekends, still getting good support from local customers but the volume of trade, like the cash flow, slowed to a trickle.

Most of our leisure was spent quietly cocooned, enjoying homely pleasures denied us in the summer. My mother joined us for Christmas; a strained occasion for all of us, in a strange place, with so many loved ones gone. Early in January, we bought tickets for a New Year dinner at Castlepoint, a small family hotel with a wonderful view of the mouth of the harbour. It would be attended mostly by hoteliers and traders, like ourselves, relaxing while they could.

There were few faces unfamiliar to me and I settled happily at our table with a group of friends. The atmosphere was, I thought, a little stiff, but would ease with the help of food and alcohol. The meal had not begun when John left me, perhaps to fetch something from the bar, I can't quite recall. I was startled when he came back, as he gripped me by the arm, pulling me to my feet. 'I want to leave, now.'

I was stupefied, then one of my friends spoke in a sympathetic tone: 'Have they been saying nasty things?'

He stared at her and said in a cracked voice, 'They said I murdered them.' He tugged at me. 'Please, I want to go.'

He sat next to me, shoulders hunched, head sunk on his chest, while I drove the short distance home. Indoors, he made for the bedroom and lay huddled into a tight ball. Struggling with my own misery and disbelief, I knelt by him.

'Who said it to you?'

'Oh! I don't know! Some men in the bar.'

Weeping now, he took my hand and squeezed it hard.

'I'm not going to let them take away what I have found.'

'I don't understand what you mean.'

'I'm not going to let them take you away from me.'

We carried on as before. There was nothing else we could

do. People who came to the restaurant were not noticeably different in their attitude towards us, in fact they seemed to be getting used to having John around. In shops and in the street, I received the usual friendly greetings, but it was impossible to know what they were thinking, whether they would really have preferred to avoid me.

Once, a man came to the Galley in the afternoon, before we opened, asking to see John. I fetched him and they sat near the big window, talking, for about an hour. When he left, John told me he was a cousin of Pat's, inquiring about her.

Not long after, a policewoman called on me, an outcome, I assumed, of the cousin's visit. 'We are trying to locate Pat Allen. We just want to be sure that she's OK. Do you mind answering some questions?'

'I don't know much, but I'll tell you what I know.'

She smiled and took out her notebook. I explained that I had no more idea than John had about where she'd gone.

'Where are the children?'

'They're in Bournemouth, living with one of John's aunts.'

'Can you tell me where?' I couldn't, but John's mother would be able to tell them.

She finished her tea and thanked me. I didn't find it particularly pleasant to be questioned by the police, but she had been nice. No doubt they would send someone to see the children; maybe even hear news of Pat and be satisfied.

In March, we went on holiday with Stephen and Lorna, but without Catherine, who refused to come. I arranged for her to go with her grandmother to France on a town-twinning excursion.

It was one of those package deals, with entertainment organised for children, leaving the adults free. As I lay on the beach or strolled with John around the ancient Spanish town, I found myself free to worry about Catherine and about the evil rumours circulating at home, and to grapple with a growing sense of foreboding.

John was as carefree as any other holidaymaker. I kept my feelings to myself; to discuss them with him would be to disturb his peace of mind and cause him to doubt my loyalty.

Preparations for the 1976 season began as soon as we got home. Most of the old hands remained or came back, but there were new people to be taken on, painting and cleaning to be done. Easter came and went without mishap, a routine start to the year, except for the way I felt. I was waiting for something. I didn't know what, but I knew it was coming and I feared it.

I was upstairs lying on the sofa one afternoon, not sleeping, unable to read, when the baker's wife came up the back steps and into the room. 'Eunice,' she said, 'I was hoping to find you on your own. I wanted to tell you before you hear it from someone else. The police are out at Hangar. They have got men going down inside the reservoir, looking for bodies.'

Was this what I had been waiting for? I felt my stomach lurch and the weight of dread grow inside me, but no, this was not it. I didn't move. She went on: 'My mother-in-law is very annoyed about it.' As though my dog had peed on her carpet, I thought.

'Well,' I said at last, 'they are wasting their time. They won't find anything.'

John's reaction when I told him, though cooler, was much the same. 'They won't find anything,' he said.

For the next few days I went about my work like someone incubating a deadly disease, sick but not yet able to name the malady. On Saturday of the Spring Bank Holiday, we were as busy as we could hope to be. I had run upstairs to the cupboard where we kept back-up stocks of wine and was searching for a particular bottle, when I was overwhelmed by a feeling of impending doom. I leant my head against the racks and prayed. 'Please God, whatever is going to happen, let it happen soon, so that I can have it behind me.'

I felt my prayer had been heard. It was the last time I was

to receive such solace. After that, God was out when I called.

On Sunday morning, at about half-past-eight, I was dragged from my half-waking state by an insistent knocking on the front door. I heard Catherine run down to answer it. On the landing, struggling into my dressing-gown, I met her coming back, her face a mixture of alarm and embarrassment.

'It's the police,' was all she had time to say before the stairs behind her were swarming with men. At the periphery of my vision, through the open bedroom doorway, John was raising himself in the bed. I retreated to the living-room. Officers in plain clothes were dispersing around the flat. I saw that there were some women among them.

The short, heavy man, who appeared to be in charge, formally addressed me: 'We want you to come with us.'

I can't be certain of what came next, perhaps 'to answer questions', or 'in connection with', but the closing phrase hit me like a hammer blow, 'the homicide up the road'.

Homicide! Had they found a body then?

Dazed, I went back to the bedroom to get dressed. Two policewomen followed me. The room was empty.

'Where's John?' I asked.

'John's gone.' This was spoken kindly but with absolute finality.

I put on the first clothes that came to hand; jeans and a loose, linen sailing smock.

There were fewer people milling about when I came back to the living-room; some of them had clearly left with John. It was explained that two women would stay with my children while I was being questioned, while the remaining men were going to search the flat.

Lorna came to me; could she go to play with her friend Sally? She seemed unruffled, confident that there was nothing amiss. I glanced at one of the women. She nodded. That would be OK. 'All right, take your anorak.'

At the point of leaving escorted by two, perhaps three people – I was too bemused to take everything in properly –

we were stopped by one of the officers detailed to search. 'Eunice,' he said, 'can we have your keys, and how do we get into the attic?'

His friendliness struck an odd note in this frightening situation. I found the keys, spent a minute or two explaining which fitted which door and showing him the trapdoor to the roof space, before I was ushered to a waiting car.

I was taken to Kingsbridge Police Station. The interview began in a small office, downstairs I think. The short, heavy man, Detective Superintendent John Bissett, was there ahead of me. He sat behind a large desk, a sergeant, whose wife I knew quite well, sitting at the side of the room, poised for note-taking. On the wall, just to the right of the chair which I was invited to take, was a picture, blown up to life-size, of Pat Allen. It looked like an enlargement of a studio portrait, the blonde hair professionally styled, her face carefully made up.

I was given a moment to take stock, then the superintendent asked, 'Did you know Mrs Allen?'

'Yes. I met her a couple of times.'

'What did you think of her?'

'I liked her. I found her very down to earth, very forth-right.'

'Is that a good picture of her?'

Was this some kind of test? I turned in my chair and studied the picture carefully.

'Yes, though when I saw her she didn't look exactly like that. Not quite so well groomed.'

'Did you know about this?' He spread a newspaper, or it may have been a photocopy, in front of me. It was a long, detailed report of a court case. John's trial, but it had nothing to do with dishonestly handling mail. This was an earlier trial, at Manchester Crown Court, in which he was charged with bigamy.

I began to read, too aware of the men's eyes on me to more than dimly comprehend what was written. He had left his wife and two young sons after being caught defrauding his employer and had gone to Beachy Head in Sussex to attempt suicide. He wrote a farewell note, left it with his pile of clothes and swam out to sea. After swimming some distance, he changed his mind. He went ashore on a golf links farther along the coast, got into the clubhouse unseen and stole money, clothing and a cheque book from the locker room.

My eye skimmed on. He had gone north, changed his real name, Anthony John Angel, to John Allen, and had met and bigamously married Pat in the spring of 1968. They had later married legally, once his divorce became absolute. He asked for 116 other offences to be taken into consideration. He was given a two-year suspended jail sentence. The pretty Mrs Allen held his hand in court, declared her determination to stand by him and make a fresh start. This was just too much. I closed my eyes, trying to blot out everything else so that I could grasp its meaning. The men waited.

Meeting the superintendent's eye, I said, 'No, I didn't know any of this.' I explained what John had told me about the imprisonment for the mail offence and the declaration of bankruptcy because he couldn't meet his mortgage payments.

'That much is true,' he confirmed.

'He told me he had been in the army for eight years.'

'Yes, he was a good sergeant in the army, didn't get into any trouble until he came out.'

His tone was easy, almost chatty. Getting to my feet in response to his polite request that I go to another room to make a statement, my legs surprised me by threatening to refuse to hold me up. I made it up the long flight of stairs to a room where two women waited for me. There must have been a man present at least for part of the time, though I can't remember exactly. Certainly it was a man's voice that said, 'Pat Allen is dead. We know that.'

'No. She can't be.'

'She's dead. We know that for certain.'

It wasn't true and I knew it.

'No. I just don't believe it.'

The questioning began. Not threatening, both women asking, prompting each other. They covered every detail of the time since John and I met. When we got to my father's death and I said, 'He had a coronary four days after Charles' funeral, but it took him four months to die,' the one making notes closed her eyes and shook her head in sympathy.

It went on all through the morning. They told me the children were missing. They had been to see John's mother. She knew nothing about it, had never come to collect them. No aunt was caring for them. There was every reason to fear they were dead. Superintendent Bissett came in to check progress. He looked over the writer's shoulder.

'We're taking down the stuff about John buying the pony for the kids,' she told him.

'Yes,' he said dubiously, 'yes, get it all down.'

At lunchtime, Dave Warren, my familiar Salcombe copper, appeared and offered me food, but I couldn't eat.

'Come on,' he said, 'have something. You've made enough cups of coffee for me.'

I accepted coffee. At one point in the afternoon, still refusing to believe she was dead, despite their repeatedly telling me she was, I exclaimed, 'If he had done what you say, he'd belong in Broadmoor, and I wouldn't do anything to stop you putting him there.'

Then a new thought occurred to me. 'Unless you think I helped him to do it.'

No one answered to confirm or deny it and I realised for the first time, that that was probably what they thought.

By about 4.30 I seemed to have convinced them that I knew no more than I was telling them. The interview finished and Dave Warren came in to tell me they were going to drive me home.

'I'm going to get your brother to come over and stay with you,' Dave said.

'There's no need, I'm all right.'

'Just the same, I'll get him. Tony won't mind.'

Tony didn't mind, but there was nothing he could do and I convinced him it was OK to leave me alone. I don't remember how the evening passed. The children must have been there. I didn't go down to the restaurant, Judy managed by herself. I know that as soon as I could, I shut myself in the bedroom, my mind operating on two clear levels, one churning over the events of the day, the other detached, observing my own reactions. I was cold, a chill sensation across the small of my back, as though an ice-pack had been laid there.

'I must be in shock,' I thought. I took a hot-water-bottle to bed but could find no comfort. Sentences, phrases heard in the day, reeling and unreeling in my head. Strangely, the one word that hadn't been mentioned surfaced in my brain and kept me from sleep. 'Murder.'

14

Press Harassment

On the day after I was held for questioning, I was allowed to see John. My spirit, deadened by an excess of weeping the night before, was further flattened by the sight of him. I had been shown into a small room where John was already waiting, with the police sergeant in attendance. He stood up when I came in, his broad shoulders drooping, arms crossed defensively across his chest. I saw that he was without shoes.

'You don't believe I did this, do you?' he asked.

'No. I know you didn't.'

'They tell me you've finished with me.'

'Yes. You've told me so many lies.'

Our talk was brief and bitter, uninhibited by the watching sergeant and the arrival of Superintendent Bissett.

'Do you want me to get you a solicitor?'

'He doesn't need one,' said Mr Bissett.

'Yes,' said John, 'I'd like to see one.'

'Is there anything else you need?'

'I'm cold. Could you bring me a sweater? And a cross-word?'

Blinded again by cursèd tears, I made for the door. I walked down the main street to the newsagent's and bought three papers, pens and a notepad. I called at my solicitor's office, found he was unavailable, then drove back to the Galley to fetch the sweater.

I phoned the solicitor from home, explaining what had happened. He was decisive. There was nothing he could do, being too involved. 'Unless,' he said, 'they are going to arrest you.'

No doubt it was a reasonable thing for a man of his profession to say, but for me, turning for help to a friend, the implication that there might be grounds to arrest me, was a cruel, cold slap in the face.

By the time I got back to the police station with the things for John, he had been moved to cells in another town.

My mother could be relied on too make a down-to-earth assessment of any situation. I went to see her, partly from my need to talk and partly to prepare her for the publicity that I knew must come.

Her summing-up was not long in coming.

'No, he couldn't kill his kids. She's got them with her somewhere.'

'But why would he lie about his mother taking them to Bournemouth?'

'Oh I don't know, love, but I don't believe he could do a thing like that.'

'Neither do I, but he'll have to go. He's told just to many lies.'

'All right. Get rid of him if you want to, but don't do it while he's got this hanging over his head.'

'You think I should wait?'

'Yeah. It's a terrible thing to be accused of and now they're gone, the poor sod's got nobody.'

It was an aspect I hadn't yet cooled down enough to consider.

Dave, the policeman, called in the afternoon. Over tea it was possible for me to talk, to ask questions. He told me about police efforts to trace the family. They had been extensive; checks on passport offices and foreign embassies which had yielded nothing. No school had received applications for places for the children; no claims had been made for social-security benefits.

I pressed him for his personal opinion but he would not be drawn.

'What do you think is going to happen?' I asked.

'Well, if there's enough evidence, he'll be charged with murder.'

'What? Without a body?'

'There are precedents for it.'

'You do realise he would have had to kill her one night, get rid of her body, kill the kids on the next night, then get rid of theirs; all without being seen and you know you can't sneeze in this town without everybody knowing.'

'That's true,' he conceded, 'I tell you what though; it's bloody mysterious.'

'I'm not arguing about that.'

As he got up to go, I asked, 'What's going to happen to John now?'

'It looks like they're going to have to let him go.'

'When they do, I'll come and pick him up.'

The call came from the police station at about nine o'clock. The time allowed by law to hold a suspect without charge had expired and John was being released. I drove in to fetch him. When I arrived, he was receiving instructions from the officer at the desk, nodding his compliance. While I waited, the sergeant who had taken notes at my interview with Mr Bissett came to speak to me. 'You be careful,' he said, 'you could be in danger.'

'He won't hurt me,' I said.

John followed me to the car like a docile dog and hunched himself into the passenger seat. We were well on the road back to Salcombe before he spoke: 'Where are you taking me?'

'Back to the Galley. I've got nowhere else to take you. You sleep there tonight and we'll see what you want to do in the morning.'

I parked in my reserved space in the town car park, about five minutes' walk from home. It was quite dark by now and no one saw us as we walked back down the creek road, along the quay to Fore Street, in at the side alley and up the back stairs to the flat.

I left him for a while to release Judy and lock up. When I came up, it was about midnight and he was lying awake in the four-poster.

He started when I came into the room.

'I'm sorry,' he said, 'I just climbed in here without thinking. Where do you want me to sleep?'

I hadn't thought about it either.

'Oh stay where you are. I can sleep on the sofa if I want to.'

In the end, I lay down beside him. It didn't matter. He sank into the bed as though he had been flogged, there was no question of touching. We talked, or rather he did. I was waiting for some explanations.

Pat had come back for her children. It must have been the day after I had been at the flat and helped to put in the ear drops. 'I was sitting on the sofa and she came up behind me,' he said. 'She looked stunning. New clothes, hair just done. She said she couldn't live without the kids and she wanted to take them with her. I seemed to be the best thing for everybody. I gave her £70, all the money I had, to help her on her way. I carried the case to the car, kissed the kids goodbye and watched her drive up the road. Her boyfriend was waiting for her somewhere.'

'Why didn't you tell me this? Why let me go on thinking they were in Bournemouth?'

'I meant to take them to Bournemouth, but then Pat turned up. I thought you'd be happier if you thought they were there near their grandmother.'

'Happier than knowing they were with their mother?'

'Better than thinking they'd been taken off to America or Canada with a man they didn't know.'

It was a poor explanation, but he seemed to think it satisfactory, apparently seeing nothing dishonourable or insulting to me, in creating a fable that I might find more pleasing than the truth. I'd had enough for one night.

'Well,' I said, 'unless you've got a better idea, I'm taking you to Bournemouth tomorrow.'

He raised no objections to my scheme until we were approaching the end of the narrow lane that runs north from Kingsbridge, between high hedges, to the A38, the spine road linking Exeter with Plymouth and Cornwall. With half a mile to go to the slip road, he began to plead with me not to break off our relationship.

He was a good advocate, arguing that his every instinct was to be upright and honest, that he'd made stupid mistakes for which he'd paid dearly. He pointed out that had he not had a criminal record, even though it was only for petty fraud, the police would probably not have given a second thought to Pat's walking out on him.

Though I was inclined to agree with that, I refused to be swayed. He had to go, but now he protested against going to Bournemouth, arguing to be taken to Plymouth. I was against it. Plymouth was too close and he had no friends there. I wanted to dump him on his mother, who could at least provide a safe haven while he sorted out this latest mess. A decision had to be made before we reached the dual carriageway. I pulled to the side of the road.

For an hour or more we argued, until I saw that it was useless. He would counter point for point to his last breath. I could not compel him to go to his mother. I started the car and turned left for Plymouth.

We found a small boarding house with vacancies near the Hoe. Without waiting to see him inside or to get a telephone number, I left him.

Connie and I had for years taken turns to phone each other on Sundays, but this week I made the call early, to tell her what had happened and to warn her that there was likely to be a lot of publicity.

'Do you think it will make the national papers?' she asked.

'Yes. I think you have to be prepared for that.'

I explained John's departure to Judy and the others. Most people were polite enough to refrain from comment, but not all. One wealthy woman who had been a regular client since long before Charles died, came in as hostess to a large party during the week that followed. She enjoyed a successful evening, her guests happy and talkative, but as she passed me the plate bearing her credit card, she told me loudly that she would not be coming again. She couldn't possibly patronise a place where there was no man around.

At some time during that week, the police held an unusual press conference at their headquarters in Exeter. Every detail of John's past was revealed and their grave concern for the safety of the mother and children emphatically expressed.

It was timed so that the first reports would be in the papers on the Sunday of the Spring Bank Holiday, almost exactly a year since Pat was last seen. They hoped, it was explained to me later, that many of the people who had been visiting the area then would be back. Malborough was holding its fête again; memories might be jogged. They wanted to hear from anyone who might have seen Pat or the children after that day.

The story was carried prominently in every paper, mostly on the front page and on local and national radio and television news. Headlines were in varying weights of type and size according to the tastes of the particular readership. Every paper had photographs. The one I had seen in the police station of Pat and snapshots of the children in a swimming pool, little Vicky in her inflatable armbands. Oddly, there were none of John. I didn't see every paper on that Sunday morning, but the one that dropped through my door bore, black and large, the words: 'Police step up search for vanished wife and children.' Nothing too sensational, but they had the effect of skewering me through the gut and it was to get much worse. My name was mentioned only to say that John had come to work at my restaurant and that we were living together, leaving those who hadn't already done so, to come to their own conclusions about my part in the affair.

The instinct to crawl away and hide could not be indulged, the work of the restaurant had to go on and without John, there was more for me to do. I was loading rubbish bins and sacks into the back of the car, there being no municipal collection at bank holidays when it was needed most, when Catherine came round the corner, returning from her job caring for the small son of a hotelier.

She had seen the papers. Her pain was visible, but I as perpetrator could offer no comfort. She asked if I had seen them. I nodded and shrugged to indicate that it had to be endured and she passed me and went into the house. On the corner opposite, the hoarding outside the newsagent's read: 'Scandal hits Salcombe'.

A reporter from the *Western Morning News* phoned and asked to see me. I agreed and he came to the Galley. In my living-room I answered the by now predictable questions. I also told him that John was staying in a boarding house in Plymouth.

His report, which appeared the next day, I might have found acceptably accurate had I been in a less hypersensitive state, but as it was, I thought I had been misquoted, some remarks omitted and some taken out of context. I concluded that it was not safe to talk to the press and resolved not to do so again, a resolution strengthened when John rang from Plymouth to say that he would have to move on. Reporters had found where he was staying and were besieging his land-lord, who took a pretty dim view of it. He was going to Bristol to escape them.

For me, there was no escape. I don't know how many reporters descended on Salcombe, maybe not more than a dozen, but they lay in wait for me, watching from the café opposite, so that I couldn't venture into the street. I had no way of knowing which of the people who came through the door were customers and which were from the press.

Judy was a source of strength and support. She fended them off. Once she came upstairs with a card. Penny Hart of the *Sunday Express* requested an interview. Perhaps it would have been wise to see her, it might have eased the pressure from the others, but I couldn't take any more. I got the impression that Judy thought I should talk to her, but I refused.

I didn't go to work in the restaurant during opening hours, staying upstairs in the flat while Judy ran things. One afternoon I was in the restaurant kitchen when a man came in and spoke to her. It could have been someone making a booking, but she came to find me, saying it was another reporter asking to see me. I shook my head and she returned to give him the message. I heard him slam out, shouting over his shoulder, 'Right! The war is on.'

An empty threat. No law said I had to speak to the press, but they managed to imprison me and make my already wretched existence more uncomfortable.

I did get cornered once. At about a quarter to seven, I went down to the bar to see that everything was OK. Judy was there in readiness. Catherine was sitting on a bar stool drinking a coke bought for her by one of the few other occupants, a tall man in a brown jacket. He offered me a drink which, foolishly, I accepted, thinking he was a customer waiting to have a meal.

I had taken a sip or two when he said, 'Where's John Allen gone to get away from the police?'

'He isn't hiding from the police.'

'Why isn't he here then? And where is she?'

I could have just walked away, retreated back to the sanctuary of the flat, but it would have meant leaving my daughter in the company of this reptile.

'Catherine,' I said, 'finish your drink and come upstairs.'

She didn't hurry to obey me but sat smiling as she always did when she wanted to hide her embarrassment.

'Where is she?' my tormentor persisted.

'I don't know where she is.'

'Oh come on! You must do.'

'If you don't get out of here right now, I'll get you thrown out.'

I had a momentary vision of the chefs coming to my rescue with meat cleavers, but it didn't come to that. He tossed back his drink and left. It's possible that he was not a reporter, just someone trying to satisfy his curiosity.

John rang me, as he had been doing every night, at about 6.30. Perhaps I wanted to keep a lifeline open for him or maybe I could not subdue my need to hear his voice, but I had not discouraged him from calling. We had talked wearily, speculating on whether the police might have tapped my line, regretting that it was unlikely; it might have confirmed that we were not conspirators in a triple murder. He had been depressed, but coping. There were no plans to meet. No plans beyond how to get through the immediate crisis.

This night, early in the week that the story broke, his despair alarmed me. His second day alone in a Bristol boarding-house was coming to an end. He'd done nothing about finding work. The wavering voice betrayed his stress and in a while, his effort to hold it steady failed and a quiet, hoarse sobbing came to me over the phone. 'Please let me see you. Please.'

'All right. Come to Plymouth tomorrow. I'll meet the train.'

At 8.30 the next morning, I was waiting for him. His appearance when he came through the glass swing doors of the station concourse was dreadful. He was almost dishevelled, pale and hollow-eyed. I couldn't believe how much weight he'd lost in little more than a week. It appalled me to see tears start to spill when he saw me. I took his hand and drew him towards the cafeteria. 'Let's have a cup of coffee and something hot to eat.'

I found a table where he could sit with his face to the wall, so that nobody would see his distress, and brought food for us both.

When he was calmer, I took the only course that suggested itself to me. I took him home to Salcombe.

15

Papering Over the Cracks

How long I kept John upstairs in the Galley like a stowaway, I can't exactly recall. It can only have been for a night or two, before I finally deposited him with his mother.

Kitty was a feature writer's dream of an old mother with a wayward son. Five feet nothing tall, with a cloud of snowy white hair she exuded a genuine sweetness. Widowed for nearly twenty years, she earned her living from home, as a dressmaker.

John had seen her only a few times since his failed suicide attempt. For a year, while he was on the run from the police, she had believed him dead. His first wife, Monica, had brought the two little boys to live with Kitty when she lost her home through John's bankruptcy. Between them, they had raised the boys, Kitty caring for them while their mother retrained as a teacher.

Monica's understandable bitterness and hatred of John prevented him going to the house and restricted any kind of contact with his mother, even after she had forgiven him. Our visit now was only possible because Monica had re-married a few months earlier and moved away.

She gave me a generous welcome and hugged John, exclaiming at how thin he was. Talk turned to our predicament. Kitty's attitude to the reporters was robust. 'I soon cleared them away,' she said, 'I told them, the whole thing's ridiculous.'

'Have they gone?' I asked.

'They come back sometimes and sit in a car over the road, but I don't take any notice of them.' She turned to John. 'Where do you think Pat can have gone, dear?'

'Oh Mother, please,' his cry was anguished, 'I've just had days of this with the police.'

'Darling, I'm sorry, of course you have, I won't ask you any more.'

John got up and left the room.

'Oh dear,' said Kitty to me, 'it's awful, but it is all rubbish. Even Monica, who will never get over what he did, says he didn't do this. He wouldn't hurt a fly.'

I returned to Salcombe, reflecting that John had passed from the care of one woman who loved him to another, the difference being that everyone found her devotion totally understandable. Mine was baffling, even for me.

The lurid publicity bothered John far less than it did me, though compared with his starring role, mine was only a bit part. 'It's a nine-day wonder,' he said during one of our nightly conversations. 'Something else will come up and they'll leave us alone.'

Nine days had already elapsed and half the phone calls were still from the press, trying to persuade me to talk to them. I had to answer all the calls, as they included those from customers making table reservations.

Currently the papers and news bulletins were carrying the story and pictures of sniffer dogs at work in North Sands Valley and in the garden at Powderham Villa. The *Daily Mail*, under the headline 'Seabed Hunt for Lost Wife', reported that the Navy were likely to join the nationwide hunt for the vanished family. The police, who now feared that the mother and children could have been thrown into the sea, were considering calling in experts with knowledge of tides and weather conditions to chart where the bodies might have lodged.

John and I decided between us that it would be a good idea if he gave a statement to the press. It might help to take the pressure off me and off his mother who was also under siege. He chose the *Observer*, for no other reason than that he liked it and felt it could be trusted to quote him accurately.

When the *Observer* story came out, its author stated that John was staying at an hotel in Cornwall, though I have forgotten where and how he got there, a lapse for which I might forgive myself, considering how many other things there were to drive such details from my mind.

It began by filling gaps in the reader's knowledge of past events; John's career up to the time he came to Salcombe, the bigamy, the court cases, then went on to give John's version of events, which it did, in full. He spoke, it said, with obvious signs of stress: 'The police have given me a hard time. I know they have a job to do, but my aim is the same as theirs, to find evidence that my wife and kids are alive and well. They have been asking me every kind of question. They thought it highly suspicious that I had a boat, particularly as I sold it one month after the disappearance. Luckily, I was able to prove to them that I had said to someone months before that I was going to sell it because it wasn't exactly the kind of boat I wanted. They were able to check that. At the time I thought it was right for her to go. We had been living fairly separate lives. I did believe that she had a Canadian or American boyfriend. I had accepted that I wasn't going to be able to see the children if she took them away. She told me she wasn't going to let me have anything more to do with them. I believe her boyfriend is somewhere in the Manchester area of New Hampshire and I think that is probably where she is too. The last time she went to America, she had to leave when she was caught with an out-of-date visa, but when she came back, she said something about "I know how it's done now."

'I think that's why no one has heard from her. She doesn't want to get expelled again by the immigration authorities. She has probably entered illegally. After all, there are thousands of illegal immigrants in the States.'

Here the interviewer interrupted. What had he done to try to find her? 'Three months ago, I wrote to the American Embassy in London, asking if they could put me in touch with any newspaper or organisation that could help me in that area. They gave me the address of the British Consul in Boston and suggested I try them. I wrote there and only recently got a reply, telling me the only local paper is the *Manchester Union Leader*. There is also an organisation for tracing missing persons, like our own Salvation Army, with a New York address, that will do some investigations on payment of an international money order. I have a friend going to America shortly who is going to approach this organisation for me and also see if he can get something inserted in the *Manchester Union Leader*. I don't want her to declare herself officially or anything. I don't want to pester her. But if she would just produce a picture or something to show she and the kids were alive and well there, then it would put an end to a terrible lot of trouble.

'The police are trying to make out that I have some kind of motive for doing away with them. But that's absurd. I had a good job and a nice flat. What did I want to be rid of them for? I feel I have probably satisfied the police, but there are so many half-truths and innuendos flying about.'

'Why did she leave all her clothes and belongings, when she was such a scrupulous and well-dressed person?' the reporter asked.

'She only left the things I had given her. Anything she thought had come from me, she sorted out and left. That's what she was doing when I came home from work the night she left.'

'Was the row about Mrs Yabsley?'

'No it wasn't. It was just one of those continuing husband-and-wife things. We had parted and come together again so many times. She is a wife you could be proud to walk down the street with, but life with her wasn't easy.

'One thing I am sure of is that she would never do anything that would harm the children. Whatever she was as a wife, she was a conscientious mother.'

'Why didn't you report her disappearance to the police?'

'Because I just assumed she had gone off to her boyfriend and thought that was probably the best thing anyway.'

The report ended by saying that certain new lines of inquiry were under investigation. Hopes that it might cool the interest of the press were unfounded; police activity was providing too much rich material for the daily editions.

Dave had taken to dropping in regularly. Whether he had been officially instructed to or whether it was out of concern for me, I couldn't be certain, but he was kind and I felt him to be an ally.

In the second week of the investigation, he advised me to leave Salcombe for a while, if I possibly could.

'Things are going to hot up round here.'

Difficult to imagine how it could, they'd finished digging up John's garden, but he was obviously not going to be specific.

'I've already managed to get the kids away.' I volunteered. Catherine was going to stay with a schoolfriend in another county. She was bruised and angry because the police had read her diary when they searched her flat. Stephen was at boarding school and Lorna was going to Guides camp.

'Well, you've worried about everyone else, what about you?'

'OK. Thanks. I'll think of something.'

There were plenty of places I could have gone, but the possibility that I might be followed by the reporters ruled out most of them. I couldn't inflict that on any of my friends or relatives. In the last couple of days, I had developed an irrational longing to be alone, under big trees. I still hadn't made up my mind about where to go when John rang.

He asked if I had read the *Observer* report.

'You are variously described as "dynamic and attractive".'

He sounded amused, more cheerful.

Dynamic was not how I felt.

'Dave tells me the police are planning something big. He wants me to get away for a week.'

'A week? I'll come and collect you. I'll hire a car.'

'No. I've got to go over to Tavistock to see Stephen. He's upset because a man he thinks is a reporter approached him in the town.'

'We'll go there first, then I'll take you to my mother's.'

That wasn't a good idea either, considering the reporters camped outside her door, but it would get me away from whatever horror was about to take place in Salcombe and I was glad to have the decision made for me.

Judy agreed to take care of things with the help of Mike, a young architecture student who was working in the bar for the summer. They came up to the flat while I handed over, giving her a telephone number and arranging to call her every day. A fear I'd been wrestling with had to be voiced. 'Do you think I'm insane to be setting off across Dartmoor with a man who is suspected of murder?'

'Well,' said Mike, 'it's not something I would advise.'

Exactly. I did absolutely believe that John could not have killed them and the police had discovered nothing to shake that. It was just that it remained as a remote possibility. I had not seen Pat walk away. There was a minute but poisonous seed of doubt. Lord, I believe. Help thou my unbelief.

John met me in a small green Ford the next afternoon. I don't remember where or how we gave the pressmen the slip, but we were soon heading off towards Bovey Tracy and the Guide camp, John driving with his huge hand on his knee, engulfing mine. I had to see Lorna and the Guide mistress, to give them contact numbers in case I should be needed. That done, we turned for Tavistock.

We found a back entrance to the school in case Stephen was right and there were reporters hanging about, but we saw no one as we passed the front gate. Leaving John waiting by a little wicket gate in a back lane, I made my way to brief the head on what was happening and to see my son. A boy was sent to bring him from the showers and he arrived looking very scrubbed and vulnerable. We spent half an hour together discussing his anxieties, before I left him, I hoped, reassured.

It had all taken longer than we had thought. John produced a rug and persuaded me to lie under it on the back seat until we were clear of the school grounds. I didn't care much for the melodrama, but I lay down, too miserable thinking of my scattered children to have more than a momentary qualm about starting across the moor in the deepening twilight.

The house was in darkness when we drew up outside. John let us in with a key. Kitty had gone to bed but had left cups out on the kitchen table and my bed covers were turned down in welcome.

I went up and got into bed while John made coffee. He came in and set the tray on the bedside table.

'I want you to take these,' he said, holding out two pills.

'What are they?'

'Mogadon. I went to see a doctor in Bristol and told him about my problems. He gave me these and some Valium.'

That surprised me. I had found it too painful to talk to anyone, and the one friend who'd rung me offering support had been rather badly snubbed.

'What did the doctor say?'

'He said "You poor chap, have some Valium." Come on, take them and get some sleep.'

I did as I was told. John sat on the bed while we drank the coffee, then he tucked the covers round my chin before he turned out the light and left me to sleep alone.

I woke feeling leaden and woolly witted. John brought tea and sat beside me drinking his, having apparently decided that the moment had come to make an absolutely clean breast of everything. It was not the best time he might have chosen, I kept drifting back to sleep, but I didn't want to discourage him.

'I'd be with Monica now, probably, if it hadn't been for that,' I heard him say. 'I was doing well in the company, we'd got a new house and furniture. Our first boy was turning out to be exceptionally bright and we wanted to get him into a private school. Monica wanted a car, so I got her one as a surprise for her birthday. I parked it outside the house with a big ribbon tied round it.

'We started to get into debt. It was part of my job to make up the pay packets, so I fiddled the wages records; I took a pound out of each packet, but I got found out. When I told Monica the CID were coming round, she went mad. I couldn't stand it. I drove to Beachy Head, really meaning to kill myself. I left my clothes and swam out to sea. I was going to keep going, but I'm a strong swimmer and I just couldn't do it. I swam to a beach and got into a golf course. I took some money and clothes and a cheque book.'

I was trying hard to concentrate. Kitty came in and joined us for morning tea. He was telling me how he got a job, first in a bakery, then in a factory making washing machines, beginning to build up his new, false identity. He had changed his name to John Allen when he met and fell heavily in love with Pat.

'She was so lovely, I used to get a lump in my throat, just looking at her,' he said.

'Why bigamy?'

'She wouldn't come to live with me until we were married,' he said, as though that was complete justification. 'She would never have known if I hadn't been recognised walking down a street in Manchester. Someone saw me and told the police.'

The suspended sentence I knew about from the papers. Monica had divorced him and they had left Vicky and Jonathan with an au pair while they went off to get married, their troubles behind them.

I heard him out, through his confession of imprisonment for the Post Office offence to the day he met me, though some details of dates and places I couldn't retain in my befuddled state. His account seemed not to vary from what I had read or heard from the police, but it was enlightening to get a glimpse of the affair through his eyes.

Anxious to fulfil my every whim, John drove me to Poole Park, so that I could be under big trees. It wasn't quite the secluded glade of my imagining, but there were trees and water. There were also throngs of people, none of whom gave us a second glance, which was almost as consoling as solitude.

We sat on the grass and discussed what was to be done. He felt it would be unfair to go on staying with his mother while he was still making headline news. A live-in job was the obvious answer, but might be difficult to get in the circumstances. Then I thought of a caravan. He seized on the idea as soon as I suggested it. How much could I afford? he demanded. I couldn't really afford it at all, but thought I could find £500.

He was on his feet immediately, racing across the green to get the local advertiser. In a few minutes he was back and together we scanned the 'Caravans' column. There were plenty to choose from and we settled on a tiny, second-hand two-berth Cheltenham, light enough to be towed by the Golf. We called at the seller's house and I paid the money, but left John to arrange to have it berthed on a site near the edge of the town.

On our way back, our attention was caught, as we pulled up at traffic lights, by the legend screaming from a news-vendor's billboard: 'Sea hunt after Salcombe angler hooks heavy object'.

John pulled over and went back for the paper. I felt sick. He read the story then passed it to me, but I couldn't look at it.

'Are you all right?' he asked.

'Yes, I'm all right.'

'Yes, well, I saw your face when you read that billboard.'

By the time we reached Kitty's house I'd had time to reason that the story was just a device to keep the sensational headlines going. Whatever the angler had found, it couldn't have been Pat's body or one of the children's. They would have been in the water for more than a year and any Salcombe fisherman would tell you crabs would have eaten every last trace of them long ago. The police must be mad.

Back at the house, I made myself read the story. Police frogmen were diving in the estuary after a Mr John Mundy from Essex broke his line on a 'heavy object'. He cast his line again and landed a woman's blue handkerchief folded round some paper tissues. He threw these away, but went to the police after reading about Mrs Allen's disappearance.

Mr Bissett was quoted as saying: 'The handkerchief was still folded. It is possible that it could have been hooked out of a handbag, or even a piece of clothing. If it had been free it would have unfolded and floated away.'

The police appealed for information about a dinghy used by John to ferry himself to and from his boat. The story told how John had sold the boat and gone to live with dark-haired Mrs Eunice Yabsley at the Galley restaurant. There were details about Charles, how he'd died of a heart attack. They got the date of his death and his age wrong, then went on to quote my sister-in-law, Francis' wife: 'The family were scandalised and upset when she took up so soon with this other man after Charlie's death.'

A few words from my mother, speaking in my defence, concluded the piece. There was a picture of me and a much larger one, across five columns, of frogmen surrounded by children, assembling their equipment on the Salcombe foreshore.

'Keep out of the way for a week,' Dave had said. Still five days to go. It was impossible to relax. Kitty's large living-room window overlooked the road and though the reporters were not nearly so vigilant as the ones in Salcombe, they turned up at some point in the day and a few took turns to sit in a parked car across the road for most of the evening. They didn't seem to know John and I were there and I didn't want them to find out.

Moving about the house was difficult, there were no curtains at the frosted glass of the front door, and anyone on the stairs could be seen from outside as a distorted shadow. I kept a good deal to the kitchen at the back of the house, pressing myself dramatically against the wall to check that there was no one on the doorstep, when I wanted to go upstairs, before making a dash for it.

John almost revelled in it. It gave him a chance to practise a few of the skills he'd learned in the army. One night after dark, the car was parked opposite the house and showed no sign of moving. He decided he would put them to the test. He put on black trousers and sweater and slipped out of the back door into the street. He went for a walk on the common, passing close by the car on the way out and back. They didn't notice him.

16

Under the Surface

As soon as I got back to Salcombe, I went to the end of the ferry landing jetty to see if the divers were still at work. From there I had a sweeping view of the estuary, from 'the bag' to Bolt Head, but in fact, I hadn't far to look. About fifty yards away, close to the shore, a cluster of small inflatable boats, holding four or five men in wet suits, bobbed within a ring of marker buoys. As I watched, a frogman surfaced and hauled himself aboard.

A warm summer wind ruffled my hair and the water. The tranquillity of the harbour was not disturbed, nothing hinted that these men were searching for murder victims. To me, it was unreal, unbelievable that this should have anything, even indirectly, to do with me, that any action of mine could have brought this taint to this beloved place.

The flat was a haven of a sort, though constant traffic through the front door kept me confined upstairs and every ring on the phone carried a threat. At least it was better than walking strange streets, envying the ordinary lives I glimpsed through lighted windows.

Complete isolation was impossible. I had to know what the papers were saying, though reading them was painful. One report might have made me smile if its implications hadn't been so sickening. A Salcombe informant who kept in regular touch with the press had seen me helping John move his belongings out of his flat or may have simply passed on a juicy piece of pub gossip. The headline read: 'The Mystery of the Brass Bound Trunk'.

National and regional news on TV kept viewers up-to-date with the investigations. On *Nationwide*, a representative from the Salvation Army's bureau dealing with missing persons inquiries was interviewed. The report opened with shots of Powderham Villa and some introductory remarks from Frank Bough about people who vanish without trace.

The Salvationist was asked what the chances were of tracing Mrs Allen. He gave details of their success rate and the numbers of cases dealt with by his organisation every year. The *Daily Mail* also carried national statistics. In the year before, 5,000 people had been reported missing; 3,000 cases remained unsolved on police files; 70 per cent of missing persons turned up eventually.

The next time I was summoned for one of my regular visits to see Mr Bissett, I pointed these facts out to him, though doubtless he knew them already.

'Yes,' he said, 'but it's not easy to disappear with two small children. You can't say to a little kid of four or five "Your name is not Jonathan any more", and we've contacted every school in the country. No children with those names have been registered.'

I put his point to John when he phoned.

'I don't suppose they've checked every private school,' he countered, 'or every school in America.'

There wasn't much doubt about police opinion of the fate of the family. A 'senior detective' had stated quite openly that: 'All our efforts have so far not met with any success. There are still a few leads to check out, but we have to face the fact that it is now a probability that we have on our hands a series of murders.'

Headlines grew ever more lurid. On 4 June, across the front page of the *Salcombe Gazette*: 'Mystery Grows in Hunt for Family', with subsidiary headings, 'Grisly Task' and, in bold capitals 'LATEST FIND A PIECE OF FLESH'. A local fisherman, who wished to remain anonymous, handed a piece of flesh to Detective Superintendent John Bissett, who sent it to the police forensic laboratory for analysis. On the advice of a clairvoyant brought in by the police, divers were now concentrating their search between the Black Rock and Wolf Rock.

Another picture of the diving team occupied the centre of the page, beside it a two-year-old picture of me and Charles sitting together on the long window seat of the restaurant and at the foot of the page, an outside shot of the Galley, showing the hanging sign.

I had taken the paper to read it in the bedroom. After the first paragraph, I threw myself face-down on the bed, gasping with horror. It was several minutes before I could read on.

'The scandal has shocked and angered the people of Salcombe, mainly because it has implicated Mrs Eunice Yabsley, the widow of Charlie Yabsley, who was one of the town's most popular characters. More than 600 people attended his funeral in January last year.'

Were the people angry on my behalf, I wondered, or was it because I was a piece of Charlie's property?

There was more. 'Shortly after Mr Yabsley died, Mr Allen went to work at the Galley, Mrs Yabsley's restaurant. Within a few months Mr Allen and Mrs Yabsley were living together and running the restaurant between them. Then,' it said, 'Mrs Allen disappeared.'

This last phrase incensed me. It was untrue, though possibly I was the only person to appreciate the fine deviation from the facts. John and I did not start living together before Pat vanished. Almost two months elapsed between her walking out and him moving in with me. The inference could be drawn that she disappeared as a result of John coming to live with me. If I'd had enough drive and determination left to do anything about it, I would have sought to sue for libel. As it was, I barely had the spiritual strength to get up in the morning.

I thought of those women in biblical times 'taken in adultery'. I was being publicly stoned for mine. 'Thank God,' I thought, 'it's not three hundred years ago, they would have dragged me out and burned me at the stake.'

My burden became almost too much to bear. I entered an arena of despair in which I came to know myself. The prospect of being a key witness in a sensational murder trial was something for which I could not begin to prepare myself. The inner strength which had always sustained me, I saw was an illusion. Faced with what was, for me, the ultimate test, to withstand public degradation, my personality threatened to crumble. I found myself wanting in courage; weak and vain. The revelation changed me profoundly.

Friends were kept at arm's length for fear they might see through the façade of dignified calm I tried to present. I might have been able to talk to a total stranger, but those whose good opinion I valued, I kept at bay.

The doctor who had tended Charles at his death arrived unsummoned one afternoon when the scandal was at its height. He dropped into an armchair. 'Stephen came to see me,' he said. 'He's worried about you. He says you're not sleeping.'

I was touched, though how my thirteen-year-old son knew it, I didn't understand. It was a clear invitation from the doctor to talk. I tried but could not bring myself to tell him of my feelings. I managed only a reference to the report in the *Gazette*.

'That was cruel,' he said.

So cruel I could not refrain from tackling the editor when I happened to see him in the shop that occupied the ground floor of the newspaper offices in Kingsbridge. There were a few customers and a couple of assistants standing about, when I stepped out of character and berated him for his annihilation of me.

'You didn't even get it right,' I shouted.

'Eunice, I'm so sorry, I was away on holiday. If I'd been here I would never have let it go through.'

It was no consolation, but he was an old friend and there was no malice in him. I believed him.

People I didn't know, who had never met me, managed to cause me grief. A friend with whom I was in regular contact because she laundered tablecloths for me, repeated a particularly disturbing story.

She had been to a flower-arranging class, held in a large house, attended by about twenty women. The tutor, also mistress of the house, by way of making amusing small talk, asked her class:

'When do you think the police are going to dig up Charlie Yabsley's body?'

The police had never hinted that they had any such intention, though in common with most other people they found it hard to believe that John and I met for the first time only two weeks after Charles died.

It was appalling. Had my children heard these rumours? Was there any possibility they were harbouring fears that I had done away with their father?

They had never given me reason to think so, though Catherine communicated with me only when absolutely forced to. The worst worry Stephen had expressed was after one of his friends told him a yarn about fingernails being washed down the gutter. Lorna, I hoped, was as detached from it all as she appeared to be, her head full of going to ballet school in the autumn.

I complained about it to the next policeman who came to see me. He listened and assured me they were satisfied that Charles had died from natural causes. Had they ever doubted it? He asked who had made the remark. I told him. For once it was possible to pinpoint a rumour-monger.

John, the cause of my torment, was my only ally. Even my mother, when she read about the bigamy, said she didn't ever want to see him again and, though she later retracted, it made it difficult to confide in her.

He was living in the caravan now, on a park in Bournemouth, near the river. He had got a job as head waiter in a small hotel. None of this was hidden from the police, but for the moment they were content to leave him alone, knowing where they could reach him.

Sometimes when they received new information, I was called in to the police station. Occasionally, officers would come to the flat for an informal chat. It could be very revealing, for me, if not for them. The WPC who babysat on the day of my interrogation told me that the investigation had been started, not as I had assumed, when Pat's cousin reported her missing, but as a response to the tidal wave of gossip that had engulfed the town.

'Why didn't John report her missing?' The inevitable question.

'Do you report someone missing after they've been to you and said: "I am leaving"?'

'Well why doesn't she come forward?'

'Maybe she hasn't seen the papers, they don't circulate to America, or maybe she's afraid.'

'What's she got to be afraid of?'

'I don't know. Perhaps she couldn't face all the fuss.'

It had occurred to me that she might know very well what was going on, and was hiding somewhere, quietly enjoying a sadistic revenge. I didn't voice the thought.

'It wouldn't have been so bad if we could have traced the children. It was so sad, seeing all the little dresses and things, she left them all behind.' There hadn't been any children's clothing left in the flat when I helped to clear it out, they must have been round the town collecting it from the people John had given to.

'She may have just left the things the kids had outgrown.'

'These were new things. And she left her sewing machine.'

She was convinced of John's guilt, but I wasn't. Why kill them even if he wanted to be free of them? Why not just walk away as he had done before? And does a woman leaving in a hurry, bother to lug her sewing machine with her?

Mr Bissett himself, accompanied by the note-taking sergeant, came to see me after Percy Diamond responded to the publicity and contacted them. We went over the deal with Percy and I handed over the jewellery I had locked in the safe.

A day or two later, a headline blazed that the police had discovered a blood-stained necklace. It was incredible. I'd seen that jewellery and beyond needing a clean, there hadn't been a mark on it. I was told what the newspapers didn't mention; that the blood was of such microscopic quantity, it could have come from a scratch or pimple on Pat's neck.

John and I needed to see each other. I drove to Bournemouth one Sunday in the sizzling heat of the 1976 summer, for an almost joyous reunion. His turn to remark on how much weight I'd lost. He had been doing a spot of carpentry, making a frame so that the two single berths could be converted to a double bed, carrying the timber precariously balanced on the tiny motor scooter he'd bought for getting to and from work.

His mood bordered on contentment. He had sought out his eldest son, the boy he hadn't seen since the suicide attempt ten years before. Through Kitty he found the bar where he had a summer job and spent a couple of evenings watching him at work before he made himself known. He didn't get the rebuff he might have expected and they arranged to meet again, though without the boy's mother knowing.

The job in Bournemouth didn't last long and we moved the caravan closer to a site in the South Hams, near Modbury. A few weeks later, the decision was made, possibly jointly or maybe in response to subtle pressure from him, for him to come back to the Galley.

Results of forensic tests on the piece of flesh found in the harbour were never published; the divers' search yielded nothing and my car had been examined in the police laboratory. Still the police had failed to produce a single piece of evidence to suggest that John was guilty of murder or that a crime had been committed at all. Things hadn't exactly cooled down but arrest and imprisonment seemed less imminent.

The return to Salcombe was difficult for us both, but I reasoned that if I believed in the principle 'innocent until proven guilty', I should uphold it in my personal life.

On his first day back, John showed his face in Fore Street, taking the mail to the Post Office. He came back saying he'd been kindly received by the two ladies who ran the Post Office. No one else paid him any attention, but he'd been spotted. It was not long before word reached the solicitor. He rang me to tell me angrily that he would not tolerate having John back at the Galley. If he did not leave immediately, he was coming personally to put a padlock on the restaurant door.

It was not to be borne. I approached a large firm of solicitors in Plymouth and asked to see someone specialising in probate and trusteeships. I wasn't sure if anyone would champion me against a brother solicitor but one of the partners agreed to act for me. I now had two solicitors, one to defend me from the other. They sorted things out quietly between them, probably over the phone, but there were no more threats to close me down.

The children broke up for the summer holidays. Catherine had already opted to leave school and was working locally. Living in the middle of the town it was easier for them to sail and to get to the beaches on the far side. There was also more contact with casual visitors than they were used to, not all of them desirable. Among their wet and sandy friends who trooped in and out of the flat, was one boy with a record of violent delinquency.

He was among a group talking and laughing out on the flat roof when he picked up Stephen's air gun and took a pot-shot through a window, at one of my neighbours as she sat at her desk, hitting her in the backside.

The boy fled when I rushed out, down the outside staircase, along the side alley, pausing to kick in the first window he passed, perhaps thinking it belonged to the Galley. In fact, it belonged to our landlord, the baker.

The baker's wife managed to restrain him from turning the hose on me when I went to apologise for the outrage. Apologies and promises to repair the damage were not enough to placate his fury. Soon, I received a directive forbidding my family to use the back entrance to the flat.

I had taken a lease for a second year but it was fairly obvious that I would not get the tenancy for a third, so I began to make contingency plans. I applied for planning permission to extend our living accommodation above the restaurant upwards into the roof and began negotiations to buy back the ground-floor front room, opening off the street, that Charles had sub-leased. The additional entrance would be useful and I could foresee a time when I might need an alternative to the fire exit which, at the moment, existed courtesy of the baker. Without a viable fire exit, I would not be allowed to continue trading.

Regatta week marked the peak of the season. Every night we were packed to capacity and kept busy all day preparing for the following night. On the morning of the waiters' race, I was working at the desk upstairs while John was unpacking boxes of wines, placing each bottle in its coded slot in the racks. There was a lot of noise. A waitress was vacuuming the stairs; outside, in the street, spectators and contestants for the race were assembling.

The noise of the vacuum cleaner stopped abruptly and the waitress came to me saying I had better go and see John. Something was wrong. I found him lying on the floor, breathless and suffering severe chest pains. He'd been unable to make us hear him so, finding the Hoover was plugged into a power point within his reach, he pulled the plug out, knowing that would bring the waitress to investigate.

We made him comfortable on the floor and called the doctor. He couldn't be certain but there was a possibility that John had had a coronary thrombosis. An ambulance was called to take him to the coronary care unit in Plymouth for tests.

It was difficult for the ambulance driver to back up to the door in the milling crowd. Judy asked the policeman who appeared at the door if he could stop the TV cameramen, there to record the race for the local news, taking pictures of John as the stretcher was manoeuvred through the doorway. He scowled and ignored her, but she needn't have worried, the photographers hadn't realised the patient was news-worthy.

I followed the ambulance in the car, knowing that what-ever the outcome of the tests, I would have to be back in time to open. Once I had given required information to the admitting nurse, I was allowed to see him. He was lying stripped to the waist, linked to a monitor. He was able to remove a face mask to talk.

'I certainly leave the Galley in some funny ways,' he said. A preliminary examination had been reassuring. The pain was probably caused by a spinal nerve becoming trapped between two vertebrae. Since it was presenting as chest pain, he was to be kept under observation overnight.

Back at the Galley that night, one of the waitresses approached me hesitantly:

'I'm sorry about John, Eunice.'

'Thanks, but they think he's OK.'

I explained the trapped-nerve theory. She looked blank for a minute.

'I thought he was dead. My neighbour told me he'd committed suicide.'

'No, he'll probably be back tomorrow, then she can see for herself.'

'I'm sorry, she'll be upset. She's not like that. She was so sure.'

My mother overheard an even more colourful version of the event. Two of her neighbours were discussing John's removal in the ambulance, their voices raised to carry across the gardens.

'There was blood everywhere,' said one, 'he was covered in it.' She wasn't sure if he'd cut his wrists or his throat. When John arrived home the next afternoon, we took a slow stroll down Fore Street, to give the gossips time to get a good look.

'It's a good job I didn't die,' he said, 'you'd have had some explaining to do.'

Sometimes I tried to remember what it was like to be bored, but return to a happily humdrum existence was a long way off. The police were managing to keep press interest alive by regularly taking the investigation along new paths. I stopped reading the papers to spare myself pain, but it was not always possible to avoid the headlines. Sitting next to us in a Plymouth coffee shop one day, a man studying the sport on the back page stretched like a banner in front of my face: 'Helicopter in Search for Blonde's Grave'.

A helicopter with a special device for detecting disturbed ground had been brought in to scan the fields of the South Hams. John was unruffled, but then, he had the advantage of being the only person around who knew with absolute certainty whether or not he had murdered them.

17

Family Life

Soon after John's return, Pat's old Volkswagen was found in the Batson Creek car park. He was called to the police station, where a map showing the tracery of creeks and inlets had been spread on a table. They showed him where the car had been found and asked how it was that he hadn't known it was there. My car, they knew, was kept in another car park, off Island Street, which runs parallel to the creek. They couldn't understand why he hadn't seen it on one of the daily trips to fetch the car.

Telling me about it, he gloated over how he'd pointed out that there is a row of boatsheds and workshops along Island Street, not marked on the map, which block the view of the creek. He couldn't have seen it from the street, nor could he explain why it was there or why there was a pair of oars sticking out of the window.

The car park at Batson Creek extends over a long stretch of reclaimed land. It is well used and the large area set aside for boat storage is always full, winter and summer. The Beetle could quite easily have stood unnoticed since the night of Pat's disappearance, though it was amazing that it took so long to come to light once the publicity campaign got underway.

An obvious explanation, that Pat had met her lover there and transferred to his car, was squashed if what John said was true and a pair of oars had been found inside.

The sinister implications, that the oars were from the missing dinghy and had been left in the car after the murderer returned from dumping bodies at sea, didn't stand up to close examination. What murderer in his right mind would set the dinghy adrift, but hang on to the incriminating oars? If he sank the dinghy with the bodies in it, why keep the oars – and how did he get himself ashore? It made no sense at all.

For months, the Volkswagen sat on the forecourt of Kingsbridge Police Station, a jarring reminder every time I drove past that the hunt was still on. Eventually, the police sergeant dropped in on us with a form for John to sign disclaiming ownership. He also told us that the decision had been made not to bring charges against him for breaking the conditions of bankruptcy. It was the first indication we had that police activity was coming to some kind of conclusion. Presumably the Beetle went for scrap.

John had regained a son but I was in grave danger of losing my daughter. Catherine was deeply unhappy, suffering I was told, from rejection, though when I tried to reach her, I was repulsed. Having foiled one attempt to run away, I agreed that she could go to live with Judy. I couldn't really stop her. Now sixteen, she had the right to live wherever she chose. ·

There were other domestic difficulties. Planning permission to build a third storey was refused, so we were faced with having to accommodate the family on the first floor, a quarter of which was taken up by the lavatories for the restaurant clients. I had managed to get back the lease of the room opening off the street, so I gained a little space, but was about to lose much more. Pressure to get out of the flat over the bakery was increasing.

John's draughtsmanship skills came in useful. He worked out that if we moved the public loos to the ground floor, we could meet all our accommodation needs upstairs, provided we used every inch of space and designed it like a caravan or a yacht.

We would have to make do with a tiny galley-type kitchen in a corner of the living room, but it hardly mattered when I had access to the restaurant kitchen downstairs. There was to be a shoe-box-size bedroom for each of the children, including Catherine, using the space formerly taken up by the toilets, and extending out across the void over the stairs. Stephen's room was so small, the only way we could get in a full-length bed was to build it like a bridge. He would need his youthful agility to get in and out. Not so easy for me, though, when it came to changing sheets.

It was to be a major upheaval, involving moving the bar and altering the restaurant kitchen to make space for the new loos. It was going to take what little capital I had, but it had to be done, mostly using our own labour. We planned to do it in the winter.

By November the season was dead and buried and we were able to satisfy my primitive urge to be under trees by taking the caravan for a week to a New Forest site near Lynd-hurst. Preparations were simple. We parked the van outside the door as soon as parking restrictions permitted and loaded clothes into the wardrobes and food into the fridge, then towed it to the near-deserted car park ready for our departure in the morning.

The rumour that found its way back to us as a result was that the caravan was absolutely stuffed with money ready for our flight from justice. For once, I found it quite funny but strangely, John was upset by it. The holiday, I think he found quite forgettable, but not the story.

After our stay in the forest, we towed the caravan to a farm close to Lorna's new school, so that we would have a base for visits and overnight stops. It was dark by the time we pulled on to the site and the owner came out with a flashlight, chatting brightly as she showed us where to park and how to hook up to the electricity and water supplies.

'Where do you come from?'

'Salcombe, in Devon,' said John, and explained that we

had a daughter nearby in boarding school.

'Salcombe? Isn't that where those two children have gone missing?'

'Yes, that's right,' said John without flinching.

'It's so sad. I don't suppose they'll ever find them now,' she said, her motherly heart wrung. I shrivelled into my shell, hoping she would put my silence and averted face down to sympathy or misery at being parted from my child.

Next morning, John drove the few miles to collect his new-found son from a renowned public school where he was in his fifth year. Diligence on his mother's part and his own brilliance had won him a place there. His younger brother had followed him, but as yet had not contacted his father.

John, visibly proud, brought him back for breakfast. I found him delightful, a tall, extremely handsome boy with dark curly hair. His pleasure at being with his father was touching, his sweetness and courtesy towards me captivating. They had so much to say to each other. If I'd had anywhere to go, I would have left them alone to talk. His fund of early memories, of times spent with his father was amazing. He had read the papers and there was a brief discussion about the scandal. It was arranged that he would come soon for a weekend in Salcombe. He came for a whole summer.

Our first task, when we began the alterations to the flat, was to reinstate the wall between us and the bakery, exactly as it had been before my tenancy. John did the job, saying he'd learned to lay bricks in the army and loved it. I thought maybe he'd learned it in prison, but didn't press him on it. Wherever he got his skills, they proved valuable now. He built me a comfortable home in an impossibly tiny space.

Finding room for a bath was a real problem. It had to be fitted round a section of the ventilation duct from the restaurant which protruded through the floor. The only way we could do it was to buy a large, expensive bath to go across a corner. John consoled me: 'You never regret your extravagances,' he said, 'only your economies.'

Time proved him right. That bath was easily big enough for us to hold our board meetings in.

I was up a ladder happily filling a cavity in a new partition wall with polystyrene balls, when my friend from the social-security department paid me a visit. Why hadn't I notified them when John came to live with me? Under their rules I was not allowed to live with a man as his wife and continue to receive widow's benefit.

The Department of Social Security had not been uppermost in my mind lately and anyway, what exactly did 'as his wife' mean? If it meant that a woman was dependent on a man for her support, then the rule didn't apply to me. I explained that John didn't support me. He was in fact my employee and, in any case, my personal tax allowance would be reduced to take account of the pension, so what was given with one hand was taken back with the other.

The man was not impressed. I felt myself becoming enraged because this little bigot was here to make a moral judgement. He would not ask me the direct question which for him would confirm my culpability: 'Do you sleep with him?' but insisted on going through his list of set questions, designed to arrive at the answer.

'Do you call yourself Mrs Allen?'

'No. I don't pretend that I am married to him.'

'Does he ever do the washing up?' Proof positive of licentiousness. I was determined to make this as difficult for him as possible.

'We live over a restaurant. We have a very large washing-up machine.'

It did me no good. Within a couple of days I was notified that all the money I had received in pension since John moved in would have to be repaid. Suddenly being faced with an enormous debt completely floored me. I lay on my bed and howled with despair and humiliation. John's reaction was interesting. He became testy and irritable, accusing me of self-indulgence. He couldn't cope with misery.

The Royal Navy made no bones about where they got their information. The letter from them began: 'In May of this year it was brought to our notice by newspaper articles that you had formed a liaison with a Mr Anthony John Allen.' They were a little kinder than the DHSS, taking away my allowance but continuing to pay me a small amount for the two younger children until they left school.

Civil servants started to come out of the woodwork. One turned up as we were heaving the huge slab of timber that formed the bar counter into its new position. He had come as a result of an anonymous tip-off that we were carrying out alterations without consent. As it happened we needed only approval under building regulations and that we had.

Except for a couple of old friends and a few new ones, the world seemed to have turned hostile. One of Charles' former drinking cronies told me to go home and watch John robbing the till, when I dropped in on him and his wife.

We were drawn closer together, becoming everything to each other, good companions and lovers, so close he couldn't bear me to be out of the room for more than a few minutes before he came in search of me. He was loving, kind and unfailingly courteous. All through that bitter winter we shut ourselves in, labouring together to get the alterations finished in time for the start of the Galley's third season without Charles.

For her eighteenth birthday present, I sent Catherine on a trip to California, to visit Charles' brother in Santa Barbara. She was gone for more than three months, spending much of the time travelling round America alone. She returned more mature, less bitter, though still hating John. She came back home to live.

John's son spent the whole of the summer she was away with us, sleeping in her room. I had no problem at all in absorbing him into the family, but I soon found I was having to defend him to John who, despite his pride and joy, was rather rigid and Victorian in his outlook. He had fathered four children but had raised none of them beyond eight years old. His expectations of early rising and hard work, I thought were unrealistic, especially in the holiday season in a town offering every delight to the thinking teenage hedonist.

More than once, John voiced regret that we would not have a child of our own. I felt no regret. I was too old and we would have fought over its upbringing. There were other ways to express our love for each other. He was always bringing me gifts, jewellery, pictures, ornaments and a silver specimen vase to stand on the bar. Every week he bought me a single red rose. I bought him a pocket watch and had engraved on the inside some lines I'd seen on an antique enamel box: 'This and the giver, thine forever.'

It is very hard to talk to a fat policeman about love. Sitting opposite John Bissett, it was difficult to imagine that he'd ever experienced it, though calling in a clairvoyant might indicate a romantic streak. Nothing else about him suggested it. As far as he was concerned, John's motive for moving in with me could only be greed. I was seen as having the sense and judgement of a Jemima Puddleduck.

He had called me to wind up our strange association. The main thrust of the inquiry was over, though investigations were still going on.

'As John himself pointed out,' he said, 'this has all cost a great deal of money, but I'm satisfied. The file is going forward to the Director of Public Prosecutions.'

It took a moment to digest this.

'Well, I suppose it must just take its proper course.' Fatalism was a comfort.

'I could have locked you in a cell,' he said. 'Lots of people would have done that. But I didn't.'

I wasn't sure if he expected me to thank him. We took our usual polite leave of each other. As I reached the door he said, 'Make sure you keep control of the money.'

The advice would have been easier to take, if it had been given at the very beginning, but John was already keeping the books and paying the wages. To try to wrest it from him now would be to admit that I didn't trust him. Anyway, to begin with, everything was fine. School fees, paying back the DHSS and the cost of alterations left us short of disposable income, but John bore that as philosophically as I did.

One of the first things he had done was end the system for the simple-minded, installed by my accountant, in which I put a percentage of takings into a separate account, in readiness for the VAT demand. He took me to task for paying bills too promptly, saying that the money should work for us for a while before we parted with it. I bowed to his superior knowledge. He had had managerial training. I hadn't.

His relaxed attitude to VAT caused me a few sleepless nights. Customs and Excise started from the assumption that businessmen were criminals and they terrified me. I always tried to keep daily records of every transaction to be sure of getting the returns in on time and avoiding the penalty. John preferred to leave it until the return was almost due then, in response to my nagging, spend a week solidly working on the books and get the return in by the skin of his, or rather, my teeth.

There had been a sticky moment in our relationship when I refused to give him authority to sign cheques and we quarrelled again when he aroused Catherine's fury by putting a sign in the restaurant window naming himself as co-proprietor. We came close to parting over that. I agreed with Catherine and made him remove the sign, but chose to have it out with him in private, thus strengthening her belief that I never defended her.

Our quarrels were rare and almost always about my handling of the children. He was dutiful as a stepfather but took no pleasure in them, except perhaps Lorna, when for a few years she enjoyed some success as a child actress.

Towards the end of her first term she had been taken by her drama teacher with a group of girls to the BBC to audition for a small part in *The Devil's Crown*, a TV series about the Plantagenets. She had rung me in great excitement. I was pleased but advised her not to get too worked up: 'They are sure to be seeing dozens of girls.'

When she rang again two weeks later to tell me she had got the part, I was ecstatic, but not more so than John.

For the several parts that followed, he was generous in freeing me to be her chaperone. Whenever we could both get away, we went together to take her for auditions, often driving through the night after the restaurant closed to pick her up from school in the morning. Occasionally he was able to spend a day watching the filming.

He had a commanding stage-like presence himself. It was a thing I'd noticed and teased him about. He was always being approached in public places for help and advice; old ladies in supermarkets asked him to find things or get things down from high shelves, which he would do, handing over the item with a little bow and addressing them as 'madam'. People tended to assume he was in charge.

At the Television Centre one day, he was walking about looking at the sets for an episode of *The Onedin Line*, holding one of the yellow camera scripts we had been handed to keep us occupied and out of the director's hair. An actor playing the part of a brokers' man came to up to him with a problem. He was supposed to burst into a tiny cottage and smash the place up, but the door was getting in the way of his axe. John considered for a moment: 'Why don't you just wedge it open?'

The advice was taken and the scene was shot with the door wedged open by the back page of John's script. Months later, watching the episode on our set at home, we could clearly see the piece of paper jammed under the door.

It was while I was away from home chaperoning Lorna, that the second of John's estranged sons came to find him, turning up at the Galley unannounced with his girlfriend. Catherine took charge, finding them corners to sleep and making them welcome. Our offspring got on well together, even if the best John and Catherine could manage was an uneasy truce. We never achieved anything like a normal family life, but there were moments of happiness in our co-existence.

Apart from a spate of articles speculating on where Pat and the children might be, which regularly appeared around the anniversary of their disappearance, press interest gradually died away, leaving us to patch our lives together. Eventually, word came that the Director of Public Prosecutions considered that there was insufficient evidence to bring a charge of murder. There would be no trial.

18

Farewell to Salcombe

We stayed in Salcombe for seven years after Pat vanished. I had expected to spend the rest of my life there but it was not to be. It was ironic, how the town seemed to have the knack of squeezing out those people it didn't want. I'd seen lots of bright entrepreneurs, thinking they'd make a killing from wealthy tourists, become restless and disillusioned by the profitless winters. I should have known John would be one of them.

By the end of the seventies recession was biting hard. John took a job out of season, with the Milk Marketing Board, recording milk yields from local farms. He antagonised a few of the farmers by doing the *Times* crossword while he was waiting for containers to fill, and standing in a pit in the direct firing line of a cow's rear end didn't have much appeal for him. He began to itch to move on.

His eldest son was now living in London with his girlfriend and when an opportunity came up to share their flat, we took it, intending to use it as a base from which to work during the week, commuting back to Salcombe to open the Galley at weekends. I thought it was a recipe for an early grave, but most of Lorna's work stemmed from London; having a city base would be good for her and might create opportunities for Stephen and Catherine.

It wasn't so easy to get work. For the first winter, John drove a minicab and I enrolled with a nursing agency. We both hated it. It was as hard as I feared it would be. Nursing had moved on; I didn't belong any more. I didn't want to be in London and I was being pressed by Customs and Excise for a VAT bill, which they claimed was outstanding and we claimed to have paid.

The idea for the second restaurant came when John saw the Barclays Bank advertisements for their crusade to help launch small businesses. They were offering 100 per cent finance to anyone who could convince them they had the acumen and drive to carry through a worthwhile project.

He saw it as a joint venture, but I wanted nothing to do with it. I was too burnt out, too sick of the restaurant business, and the discovery that he had been hiding letters from the Customs and Excise on the grounds that they would upset me, had further undermined my shaky trust in him.

He worked for weeks preparing a proposal and cash-flow forecast impressive enough to persuade the bank to loan him the money for a tiny basement restaurant in Richmond. One of the Galley's wealthy customers also lent him a large sum.

Calling his restaurant the Galley, Richmond, made obvious sense. It would reduce the start-up costs if the same bill pads and some other equipment bearing the name could be used to begin with. We rented a house in Kew to be close to his business and close to the M4 to make commuting to Devon a little easier. At my insistence, he applied to be released from bankruptcy. We went together to Stockport for the hearing and he got his discharge.

The liquor licence had to be in my name because his criminal record debarred him from holding one. I made curtains and seat covers and fought off my solicitor who refused to believe John had come by the money honestly. In return, he paid some of my more pressing bills with his new-found wealth.

When Easter loomed up again, I went back to Salcombe to make preparations, desolate at the prospect of carrying the burden alone, but I found an unexpected ally. Catherine was there ahead of me and had already spring cleaned and roped in help to paint and repair where it was needed. She worked beside me, filling gaps in the staff rota and proving an invaluable right-hand woman.

John came down every weekend, finishing service in the Richmond restaurant on Friday night and catching the midnight coach from Gloucester Road coach station, persuading the driver to drop him off at the turnoff for Kingsbridge, where I picked him up at 3.30 on Saturday mornings.

During the week, he phoned every night.

'Hallo,' I said, one midsummer night, 'do you want to hear today's disaster?'

'What?'

'The CID walked in at half-past-eight and arrested the second chef, the boy doing starters and the washer-up.'

He laughed. 'What for?'

'The British Legion in Kingsbridge was held up by a man with a shotgun. I don't know why they thought they had anything to do with it. They had to let them go.'

The story was added to our fund of amusing anecdotes about the hazards of running a restaurant, but it hadn't been funny. The police had walked in just as the place was full and taken away three of my kitchen staff, leaving me to cope as best I could. I had needed John to lean on, but he wasn't there.

Incredibly, the end of the twenty-one years' lease on the Galley was on the horizon. We had always had an uneasy relationship with our landlords, British Rail. The kindly Welshman who had been in charge of the Estates Department in Charles' day, had long gone. He had once offered the freehold, but we could never raise enough capital. When he grew tired of writing letters asking for the rent, he used to come to collect it in person and enjoy a couple of days of royal treatment from Charles.

The new management was more austere. I made the first

overtures to renew the lease about three years ahead but could get no firm answer from them. There was now some urgency. Without it, I could neither continue in the business, nor sell it as a going concern.

That season was late starting and was poor even at its height. Money was tight. People no longer came in to book a table for every night of their holiday and, as soon as the children went back to school, hotels and second homes emptied. We had scarcely made inroads into the debts built up in the previous winter and extended credit was just a memory.

Whether it was because I'd had no break after the end of last season, or because I had been withstanding stress for too long, was hard to know, but I had no heart for the job any more. When the VAT inspectors summoned me and John to discuss the disputed payment, I was in a state of black despair.

After two hours of gruelling questioning, I managed to convince them that we could neither produce proof of payment nor cash to pay again and they agreed to postpone drastic action. I had stared bankruptcy in the face before, but last time I had a bit of fight left in me.

I couldn't go on. The last place on earth I wanted to be, when November came round again, was in another restaurant. I began to gain weight. John's solution of shedding his old life and identity like a snake skin seemed very attractive; or just to have a very long sleep.

The first change in fortune came when British Rail relented and granted me a new lease. I put the Galley on the market at once, though it wasn't likely to find a buyer in the depths of winter. On the strength of the money that would accrue from the sale, John's mother lent me the money to pay off the VAT men. I didn't have to dread going to bed at night, knowing I would wake with an attack of 'night horrors', sweating, my heart's irregular pounding audible inside my head.

My kids had chosen not to come to London with us,

staying on in the flat in Salcombe so when, against all the odds, the Galley attracted a buyer in the middle of winter in the middle of a recession, they were faced with sudden homelessness.

I got a good price for it. A solicitor handled the sale and settled the debts. At the end, after twenty years of back-breaking slog, I came out with exactly nothing. Nothing to pass on to the children and nothing to buy us a new home. At least all the debts were paid, including, I presumed, the bill from the second solicitor, since I never received one. I always meant to ask for a breakdown of how affairs were settled but, rather like my reaction after Charles died, a door slammed in my mind and I couldn't bring myself to open it.

John couldn't get away to help me move out. Again, Catherine was my prop. She organised help and found some-where for me to store the furniture. She still wouldn't come with me to London. Lorna got herself a summer job and went to live-in at one of the hotels. Stephen went away to work in Bristol. In my late forties and, though I didn't know it at the time, about to become a grandmother, I was starting again, from scratch.

If I couldn't be in Salcombe, Richmond made the exile bearable. It is a pretty, elegant town with that air of ease which comes from being close to water. It held childhood memories for me from when my father had rowed us there from Greenwich. The Galley number two was a short step from the Theatre-on-the-Green, where that year the panto-mime was *Aladdin.*

Every night after the curtain came down, the cast came in to unwind, eat and drink. Carousing went on, sometimes till early-morning workers began gathering at the bus stop on the pavement above. It was punishing, but tremendous fun and kept the till ringing until the beginning of March.

On the last night of the pantomime, John conspired with the theatre management and stage hands to put on a rival performance in the auditorium. The two front rows and two boxes were booked in advance and filled with numerous friends of the cast, including a good many actors, TV presenters and producers who abound in that part of London. They were each given a copy of the *London Advertiser* and every time Widow Twanky made an entrance, the papers were opened, forming a solid wall of print across the front of the stalls.

He thwarted them. He was too seasoned a performer, trained in the northern music halls, to be thrown off balance and after the first choking laugh of astonishment, he turned the situation to his advantage, exchanging banter with the people hanging out of the boxes.

When they'd gone, the restaurant took on a quiet desolation that never quite left it. It may have been in an ideal situation for the fourth act of the pantomime, but it was just a little too far off the main thoroughfare to attract the steady trade essential for prosperity. John looked about for part-time work.

He was good at getting jobs. Employers seem to have some kind of mental image of the person they want to fill a post, rather like directors casting a play, and John managed to inspire confidence. He was taken on as a part-time negotiator for a well-known house-building firm. He did well and was soon offered full-time work.

I held the fort at the restaurant, but had no intention of taking it on permanently. It was in a shaky financial situation, with angry final demands dropping through the door and now and again a bailiff turning up at the house. I'd had all I could take of that. John never formally wound up the business, as far as I knew, he just lost interest and it fizzled out. Probably the bank took it back, I didn't ask, and John never volunteered information. I didn't even go back to pick up some of my personal possessions.

Our tenancy on the house in Kew came to an end when the owners returned from abroad and we looked for something more permanent. We made the first of many moves to

Brentford Dock, a huge development of flats on what had been a large dock for river barges, designed by Isambard Kingdom Brunel.

Our flat had a balcony with an unbelievably stunning view for London, across the marina to Kew Gardens on the other side of the Thames. For a while, we had our two sons, John's eldest, after he split up with his girlfriend, and Stephen, living with us. It was a happy time for me, but both boys moved on eventually, John's boy to a new relationship, Stephen to travel round Europe.

My efforts at finding work were not so successful. I wrote dozens of applications but never got invited for interview. I was regarded as not having worked for twenty-five years. Self-employment doesn't count and I was over the hill as far as prospective employers were concerned. I was turned down for one job in a nursing agency because I was considered too old to talk to young women. I gave up trying for a while and went back to Salcombe to stay with Catherine and her partner in their flat, to look after her when she came home with her baby daughter.

Eventually, John found me a job with his firm, beginning as a part-time sales negotiator, progressing to full-time. With us both working, we set about getting a joint mortgage on a maisonette overlooking the river on the same estate. The flats and houses had been built five years before for the London County Council's housing programme, but there had been a change of political influence in local government and the new regime considered riverside homes too good for the likes of council tenants and had reserved the most desirable for private sale.

We'd had dozens to choose from. The sales effort had been very inexpert and the flats were only just beginning to fill with new owner-occupiers. They had stood empty in the intervening years, with the central heating system fully operational. The maisonette we finally settled on was idyllic, but had been a warm and peaceful breeding ground for spiders;

we had been in residence for nearly a year before we saw the last of them.

It was a wonderfully hot and happy summer. The house was a dream. Every window looked on to the river and Kew beyond. The four-poster looked ravishing on the sanded floorboards in the bedroom, which was just as well as our budget wouldn't stretch to carpets. John's bricklaying talent was put to use again, laying paving stones in the garden and building raised flower beds and a barbecue. He was in his element. One night he looked across the table at me as we ate supper on the tiny terrace, glowing with happiness. 'I'm going to die here when I'm ninety-two, one year before you,' he said.

The gardens were divided by low walls, the right height for lolling on elbows, and each had a gate opening on to a communal lawn on the riverbank. On warm evenings, neighbours would wander along and join each other informally for drinks and a chat.

We became close to the couple next door. He was a presenter of an early-morning radio programme for the BBC and we grew accustomed to hearing references to ourselves on air. He affectionately dubbed John the 'Driller Killer', after a late session of shelf-building had deprived him of sleep. His young wife was editor of a famous weekly journal.

John was made Area Sales Manager. Comparative affluence meant we could indulge John's passion for eating out and mine for going to the theatre. I drove down to Salcombe every month or so, to see my mother and the kids. Now that I was out of catering, I looked forward to having a holiday at Easter, but the office was open to potential purchasers and I had to work. In other respects, life was beautifully ordinary, but I had almost forgotten that Easter is closely followed by Spring Bank Holiday.

John opened the door to the reporter. He answered his questions on the doorstep, but there was nothing new to tell him. There was still no trace of Pat, dead or alive. He probably would have let it pass without telling me but he thought the man had been drinking and was annoyed at not getting a story. There was likely to be a fairly vicious report in the paper next day.

He was right. To mark the anniversary of the disappearance, one of the inside pages had been given over to a full account, including details of John's past record. Within a week he was out of a job. The company directors sent for him and asked for his resignation. They assured him that my job was safe but a couple of months later, when the development on which I was employed was sold out, I was not moved to a new site according to normal procedure, but made redundant.

We were not down on our luck for long. John wrote round offering his services to several companies and succeeded in getting two job offers. He had no problem choosing between them, he accepted them both. One was for a small company in the Midlands which meant that most of his work was done from home, the other was for another house-builder and involved visiting development sites. A hard-working, skilful operator could just manage to do both. Both came with a company car.

I got a modest position selling houses as I had done before. I should have felt at least temporarily secure, but I sweated in case one or other of John's bosses found out about his dual role and he got fired again. I persuaded him to give up the Midlands job. I don't think he ever quite forgave me.

The girl next door astonished me by suggesting that I apply for a vacancy on her journal for a trainee sub-editor. At the time, I'd just received a pay rise and was getting more money for less effort than I'd ever had in my life, but the chance to retrain for interesting work was too tempting to refuse and I sent in my application, believing that at forty-seven, I didn't stand a chance.

19

Vicissitudes

Some of the credit for getting me launched on a new career John claimed was due to him, because he'd paid for me to have an aptitude analysis at a vocational guidance centre, and it had recommended that I take up feature writing. It had also suggested that I might be suited to running a restaurant but had added the warning: 'First gain experience.'

My new job meant a salary cut and a tedious journey to work, but it dug me out of a rut. Acquiring a new skill in middle age is quite rejuvenating, I felt alive and stimulated. John was less happy about our diverging paths. Picking up one of my exercises in sub-editing, on which I had marked the instructions to the printer in the required manner: '9/10pt Times Roman × 21 ems justified', he remarked, 'You are learning all sorts of things I know nothing about.'

I was changing in other subtle ways. When we had worked as a team I had never bought a pair of shoes or a piece of clothing unless he came with me and I invariably came home with not quite what I wanted. Now, I could wander down the high street in my lunch hour and, within the limits of my income, buy what I liked.

John joined a squash club and became fanatical about keeping fit. He tried hard to include me in his activities, arranging matches at centres where he could join me for a swim after his game. Once or twice I shared his morning jogs round the estate, but I had never cared for sports and I left him to get on with it, satisfying my exercise needs by walking the two West Highland terriers we had acquired in a moment of sentimentality.

My kids were still not easy in John's company, though one by one they followed us to London. Lorna announced her intention of coming to find work and I joyfully prepared the small bedroom for her, but she stayed only a couple of weeks. With her usual determination she found a flat and launched herself into teaching dance and aerobics. She was still getting film and television parts, but with less regularity. John's attitude towards her cooled noticeably.

Stephen fared worse when he came home. He could do nothing right. John had become a reformed smoker and could not tolerate even the lingering smell of a cigarette smoked hours before. Their mutual dislike deepened into loathing. I found myself once more in the agonising position of the one who loves both antagonists. When Catherine split up with her partner and brought the baby to live with us, it was a surprise that he seemed to take it in his stride. They at least had worked out some kind of truce.

For our first Christmas in the house we gathered as many of the family as we could cram under the roof. Tensions were pushed below the surface and John stepped easily into the role of genial host, presiding at the head of the extended table. His present from me was a purple brocade waistcoat which looked dazzling stretched across his well-fed middle and made a beautiful background for his pocket-watch and chain.

We had given up our bedroom to his mother and decamped to the house next door. Tidying the borrowed room before we left, John asked me to carry some of his belongings. I scooped his cufflinks and the watch into my handbag and, in the scrum of seeing off departing guests, forgot to take them out.

My mother was last to leave. We saw her off on a train from Paddington, then walked to a café in Praed Street, to

study the theatre listings in the *Evening Standard* over a meal.
I hung my bag by its strap from the back of my chair.

I realised it had been stolen as soon as I got up to leave.
The foreign staff became hostile and offended when I asked if
anyone had handed it in, thinking they were being accused.
The police at Paddington Green could only advise that I get
the locks at home changed as soon as possible.

John took it calmly, not reproaching me. We went to see
Judi Dench in a play about espionage and betrayal. I couldn't
keep my mind on her performance for fretting about my lost
keys and bank cards, but worse was the regret over the theft
of the watch with its romantic message of undying love: 'This
and the giver, thine forever'. Now someone had pinched it.
Was it, I wondered, an omen? I pushed the thought away as
silly and superstitious.

Other cracks were beginning to appear in our relationship.
Stephen told me a neighbour had seen John take a girl into
the house when I was away on a trip to Salcombe. I tackled
him about it but he angrily denied it, saying the neighbour
was out for revenge because he'd fallen behind in the
payments on a Lancia he was buying from her. I didn't
believe him, but gave him the benefit of the doubt.

I felt aggrieved because solicitor's letters were arriving at
the house, addressed to us both, demanding repayment of
the private loan to open the second restaurant, and since the
row over the car, my neighbour was refusing to speak to me.
I had not been party to either transaction but was being
dragged into the fray.

He needed to raise capital, which is perhaps why he came
up with the idea of selling the house, though he gave
different reasons. In the two years since we moved in values
had rocketed and he suggested that if we each bought a flat,
we could live in one and Catherine and Lorna could rent the
other. Stephen had by this time cleared off to a flat share.

I loved the house and didn't want to sell but my arguments
were overridden and within a few days, agents were sending

prospective buyers. The population of Brentford Dock was constantly shifting and in the middle of a London property boom it didn't take long either to sell or to find the two flats we were looking for within the estate.

Mine had a river view but only one bedroom, an advantage in John's eyes because it meant we couldn't have permanent guests. I tried to drum up a sense of pride in my ownership but I'd been spoiled. I felt like a cockroach living in a crack in the wall, but it was the best I could afford on my smaller salary. My daughters and the baby, needing more space, shared the larger flat that John bought. I paid the expenses on mine and he subsidised the rent on theirs.

He was not out of pocket because his living expenses were minimal and his property continued to appreciate at an amazing speed. The arrangement should have been to everyone's benefit but I felt he had me in an emotional stranglehold. I would have preferred the girls to be my tenants, not his, knowing he could and would evict them with very little provocation.

The easy availability of property on the dock worked to our advantage again when it became obvious that his mother could no longer cope alone in the house in Bournemouth. John handled its sale and for a time placed her in a residential home but she was unhappy, so it was decided she should live near us, where we could give her the support she needed. By a stroke of luck a tiny flat like mine became available next to Catherine.

Kitty had lived all her eighty-two years in Bournemouth. Leaving was a tremendous wrench for her, but she was encouraged by the thought that she was to live next door to her son. He allowed her to be installed before letting her know that though he owned the flat next door, he actually lived a short distance away. I thought this deception was cruel and told him so, but he argued that it had made a difficult transition easier for her.

It made her uncharacteristically demanding. Squash

fixtures and his latest moonlighting venture kept John out every evening and away most weekends, so Kitty turned to me for solace. At first, she helped by looking after the dogs while we were at work, but she didn't transplant well and became peevish, complaining about minor ills and trivialities.

I did my best to be patient, knowing geriatrics is one branch of caring for which I'm temperamentally unsuited. I listened carefully while she tried to describe the odd sensations in her head that plagued her constantly. I took her for medical checks and tried to stay sweet-tempered when I found her on my doorstep at night, waiting to unload her misery before I'd had time for a restorative cup of coffee. John saw my exasperation. 'I hope she isn't going to drive a wedge between us,' he said.

The thin end had already been driven in for me, with the sale of my pretty house on the river, and with every weekend's absence, he delivered another hammer blow. He'd given up moonlighting in favour of the water-skiing parties hosted by his friend from the squash club who owned a couple of caravans on a lakeside site. I was never invited and tolerated his neglect only because I knew how much he hated his job.

Water-skiing became his new obsession. Wet suits joined the golf clubs and squash racquets in the hall cupboard; goggles were added to the wristbands, spiked shoes, gloves with holes in the knuckles and other essential accessories.

My redundancy from the publishing company when the journal folded coincided with my final exams. I failed by a whisker, becoming the first person in the history of the journal to do so. I couldn't let failure and disappointment deter me, most people in the business had no formal training at all and mine wasn't going to go to waste. Freelancing seemed to be the course holding the best hope of long-term security and as a first step, I circulated printed cards to every magazine within commuting distance.

Work started to roll in immediately, mostly giving

temporary help with sub-editing but there were quite a few commissions for articles. Encouraged by this evidence of its benefits, John took himself off for vocational guidance. It seemed that his aptitudes were most suited for the law, but for a man of his age, that was far too long-term a project, so estate agency was suggested as an alternative. The government had just removed the monopoly on house conveyancing from solicitors.

Some of my redundancy money I had spent on furnishing my flat but the rest I tucked into a building society. It wasn't much, but it made me feel snug. When John asked if he could have a thousand of it so that he could apply for the government's enterprise allowance, I was reluctant to part with it.

He persuaded me that he could easily lose his job again the next time anything unsavoury appeared in the press. He knew how I dreaded newspaper stories. We could have been married long ago if it wasn't for the danger of attracting press attention. If he was self-employed, no one could sack him and, if she was interested, he could lift Catherine out of the single-parent poverty trap and take her into partnership.

I gave in. They rented a few square feet of office space in a converted factory and opened a conveyancing agency for couples buying their first home. Had I known John was about to become affluent I would have kept a tighter fist round my money.

Kitty suffered a stroke and died after a prolonged stay in hospital. Arranging a stylish funeral presented no problems for John but he was stumped when it came to the invitation to his first wife. According to their sons no one dared mention his name in her presence, but hers had been a closer than usual relationship with his mother and she had a right to attend.

I suggested that he wrote, beginning; 'Dear Monica, I know you wouldn't normally welcome a letter from me'. It had its effect and she agreed to come to the crematorium but not to the gathering. The boys were in a frenzy of apprehension about this first meeting of their parents for nearly twenty years, but they worried needlessly. The two came face to face for only a fleeting moment after the service, she standing beside her new husband, me at John's side.

'Hullo,' John said, 'I'm glad you came.'

She didn't answer, but looked him full in the face then turned her face to me. It struck me that she and I were very similar types. We almost smiled, but not quite.

Half Kitty's estate went to John, the remainder was divided between the boys. Understandably perhaps, no provision was made for the missing children.

John suggested we move to a larger flat. A maisonette was available in the block built above the original Brunel barge-unloading bays. It had two wonderful balconies overhanging the marina.

It would necessitate selling both our flats again and involve my daughters in another upheaval. They hadn't enough money to buy him out, but he had seen a board in nearby Twickenham, advertising the sale of flats by a housing association. The scheme was designed for people who could not afford a normal mortgage. He urged Catherine and Lorna to apply. I hated to put them under pressure but I was glad his reign as their landlord would be coming to an end.

Their application was granted but soon after, Catherine fell desperately ill. For four days she had been treated for flu but her temperature hadn't dropped below 103. The doctor was extremely irate when I called her at 5.30 in the evening. The patient herself should have rung during office hours. She didn't believe me when I said the patient was incapable of making a phone call and didn't know what time of day it was. She called, barely looked at Catherine, advised more Paracetamol and left.

The next morning she was worse. I dithered about whether to keep my freelance appointment on a mother and baby magazine. If I didn't go, I wouldn't be asked again and the mortgage had to be paid.

'I'll be all right, Mum,' croaked Catherine, 'just take the baby to the nursery for me.' I left her, but I asked John to look in on her during the morning.

At three I got a call from John. Catherine was in hospital. He'd been given the sharp end of the doctor's tongue for dragging her out again, but her attitude changed when she actually put a stethoscope to her patient's chest. 'I don't believe it,' she said, 'Girls of twenty-five don't get pneumonia.' John didn't wait for an ambulance. He wrapped her in a sheet and took her to hospital in his car.

When I arrived, she was lying on a trolley in a corridor in the casualty department. Hospital administrators were trying to empty a bed to make room for her. John was with her. 'Don't worry,' he said, 'they've promised to give her some intravenous antibiotics.' I stayed, giving her water and trying to keep her comfortable. No doctor came near. At nine o'clock, she was taken to a ward.

After a couple of days, she was out of danger, the baby's father had come from Devon to take care of her and I kept a promise to visit my sister in Aberdeen. We returned together to find Catherine recovering but still very ill. John had been in every day to take supplies of the mineral water for which she craved. When the time came for her to be discharged, I was working, so it was John who took lessons from the physiotherapist in how to percuss her back, to help clear her congested lungs.

Her tiny frame had diminished to almost nothing, she was as frail and bent as an old woman. I looked after the baby for the Easter period, to give her a few days at least of convalescence. She was still weak and sick when completion on her flat in Twickenham came up. I could do little to help because my own moving day coincided with hers.

We were both enthusiastic about the new house. I had a tiny room for a study and John equipped the guest room to double as his personal gymnasium. He installed a shower, a rowing machine, an exercise bicycle and a sun bed. He bought a video camera to record his progress at water-skiing.

The outstanding debt on the Richmond Galley seemed to have been settled; I saw no more solicitor's letters, and all was quiet on the Lancia battlefront; he sold it to a dealer. Fridays were set aside for an evening out together. I was more content than I had been for some time. This lasted about a month. My mother and sister were staying and John came upstairs trying to find me alone. He was seething with anger.

'That's it! I'm finished with Catherine. She gets her notice on Monday morning.'

It pierced me to the heart. Catherine was at that moment away in Salcombe with the little company car he had bought for her use. Things at last seemed to be getting better for her. Her own home, a car and money coming in after years of the appalling deprivation reserved for single mothers. I couldn't believe my ears.

'What has she done?'

'I turned on the word processor and I found something I didn't recognise. A letter to Susie. She thought she'd erased it, but I read it.'

'What did it say?'

'That everything was going fine, so long as John didn't get up to his old tricks again.'

I hardly bothered to try to placate him. He needed nothing less than dewy-eyed admiration from his minions. I knew he would never forgive her and I didn't want my mother and sister dragged into a family row. I kept my mouth shut but my heart bled for her.

He was ruthless in his efficiency at getting rid of her. Letters were dispatched to bank managers and the enterprise allowance board informing them that she was no longer part of the company. He showed no pity when he told her on her return that she was out. It occurred to him some days later that all this might be quite painful for me. 'I suppose you can't be happy with me now,' he said.

In her shock and despair, Catherine went to her brother. Stephen came to tell me that he wanted nothing more to do with me, unless I gave up living with John. I pleaded that I had been powerless to prevent the rift and I voiced a thought that had worried me all the time John and Catherine were in partnership: 'Don't you think it could have been her anxiety that John might get involved in shady deals that made her ill? You know she never trusted him. Sooner or later she would have had to break with him.'

He conceded this was possible and modified his ultimatum. He would never come to my house again, but I would be welcome to go to see him.

John and his son bought a small cabin cruiser and berthed it in the dock below our balcony. Sometimes on pleasant days cruising the Thames, I forgot about the enmity between John and my family, but away from the other-worldliness of the river, it tormented me. However much I liked my house, it was not my home if my kids were not welcome in it, and he was already hinting that he wanted to cash-in on the rise in house prices and sell again. I was sick of it. I longed to be settled.

On my solitary walks with the dogs, I brooded about my union with John. It was beginning to look unlikely that we would make the transition to the companionship of old age. Twelve years on I felt bonded to him as strongly as at the beginning, proving that it is possible for love to survive in the absence of total trust. The price is peace of mind. He was bored with me, that much was clear, not that he would talk about his feelings. It's doubtful that he ever analysed them himself. There was no time in our lives any more for talk. I'd always believed he should feel free to walk away, if that's what he wanted, but I couldn't discover what he wanted. He complained jokingly that I always asked him penetrating questions just as he was dropping off to sleep. I laughed with him, but it was another evasion on his part. He had put up a barricade. Lying close to me, he was a thousand miles away. I would keep a promise to myself, if I had to, that I would not stay with a man if he didn't want me.

On one of my walks, I came across the Lancia abandoned in the car park. He feigned surprise and said he would get on to the dealer to find out what he was playing at. It had never been any of my business so it wasn't worth making it into a big issue. I knew I'd been served a filleted version of the truth.

Se we drifted on. Our Friday evenings together degenerated into a quick bite at the local wine bar after his session at the squash club. The music was so deafening, conversation was impossible. Communication between us seemed to have ceased, so I jumped at the chance when he asked if I would like a long weekend in Moscow.

Plans had been in progress for a couple of days when I found he was negotiating to buy a third ticket. He wanted to take his assistant, the girl who had replaced Catherine, on the trip as a Christmas present. The original two tickets had been for them, he had been banking on my saying no.

I went on the trip, but the insult was filed away and added to the mental evidence I was compiling in my quest to know for certain his true feelings for me. The last tiny piece that I needed came when I decided the time had come to stop pussyfooting around. 'Why don't we get married?' I asked, 'there was nothing about us in the paper last Whitsun. I'm sure the press won't notice and if they do, I don't much care.'

He hesitated, looking for a suitably evasive answer, but could find none. 'Do you really want to?'

'Not particularly, and certainly not if you don't.'

He had answered my question. I tried to discuss it with him, but once again, there was no time. I made a formal appointment: 'I want to speak to you, not when you're rushing out to play squash, or rushing in to get your water-skiing gear. I need half an hour of your undivided attention.'

He looked wary. 'How about on Friday night?'

This was Tuesday. 'OK. It'll wait till Friday.'

In fact, it didn't take half an hour. We pushed our way into the crowded wine bar and ordered our food. A live pianist and vocalist were trying to drown out the noise of the jets coming into Heathrow. As soon as he settled himself beside me, I bellowed into his ear, 'If we are going to sell the house, instead of buying another between us, why don't we buy two flats? You go and live in yours and I'll go and live in mine. Well?' I added sharply when he didn't reply.

'I'm stunned,' he said, 'I don't know what to say. Can I have time to think about it?'

'Sure. How long do you need?'

'A week?'

'Right. We'll talk about it again in a week.'

A week later he still couldn't make up his mind, but he found a moment for a quiet discussion. Keeping a tight hold on my emotions I explained how I felt: 'You've lost interest in me. I'm too proud to be a bit of excess baggage.'

He gave me the lop-sided look that I recognised as the forerunner to truth. 'I suppose we have drifted apart, but I don't know if I want to split up. I've got a good life. You don't put restrictions on me. Really, I've got nothing to complain of.'

'Except boredom. Well, if you can't make up your mind after all this time, I must make it up for you. We'll split.'

20

Loves Ended, Loves Begun

For a while our relationship regained some of its lost warmth, once we had agreed to part. It was as though John was grateful to me for pushing the thing to a conclusion and sparing him the necessity of having to do the dirty on me.

We went on living together for the four months it took to sell the house. The morning kiss good-bye acquired a genuine tenderness and he took to giving me little tokens of his esteem: a porcelain vase, a lamp and, when my birthday came round, a set of cutlery.

He quickly found his next flat, on Brentford Dock of course, four bedrooms and an enormous balcony, a speculative purchase, made with the intention of taking lodgers and eventually selling after some conversion, to a family who needed a granny annexe.

My own search for a suitable place was not so simple; I had less money. We had always divided the proceeds of previous sales strictly according to what each had contributed. I got a third of the gains first time. John spent his surplus on a big car. My earning capacity had improved and now we had half shares, but he recouped the money from his mother's legacy that had been spent on refurbishment.

I got side-tracked when I went back to Salcombe for a weekend and fell in love with a flat I thought I might just afford. My longing to return set me scheming to find ways to raise a mortgage for a home in Devon while renting a room and working in London to pay for it.

John was sympathetic, doing the negotiating for me through his conveyancing business which he had moved to a plush suite of offices in Chiswick, complete with thick carpet and glamorous receptionist. It was apparently flourishing. He also suggested that instead of finding a bedsit, I might like to rent a small studio apartment which he would create for me within his flat. He drew detailed plans. I actually considered it, then realised what a silly idea it was.

Regretfully, I pulled out of the Salcombe purchase. Sale of our joint house was nearing completion and I'd wasted a lot of time. I had to start looking in earnest. John helped, keeping a look-out for likely properties, coming with me to view. He struck a deal with me; if I would agree to stay on the Dock, which I had decided I couldn't afford, I could have £5,000 more than was my share from the proceeds of the sale.

We had agreed to remain friends and he said he wanted me close enough so that he could drop in when passing. I had almost settled on an unusual little gate-keeper's lodge. I could have gazed at an open fire and been consoled for not being able to look out on water, but it would have meant a three-mile drive for him to see me and the £5,000 deal would be off.

I had known leaving John and the house on the river would be painful, but it was the first step on the road to being free from continuing pain. As moving day drew near, I stood at the bedroom window, looking across to Kew in the early morning as a narrow boat made its way down river through the mist. I wept for my loss and was angered by my own weakness. 'Stop looking out of the bloody window,' I told myself.

In the end, he found me a place, on the edge of the Dock estate, with a tiny balcony overlooking the Duke of Northumberland's park. It had a view of his rose garden and, in winter when the trees were stripped of their leaves and if the light was right, I could catch a glimpse of the river in the distance as it looped round towards Richmond.

Moving house is reckoned, with divorce, to be among the most stressful of life's experiences. They often take place simultaneously. I couldn't face the move, the seventh in eight years and decided that since it was his idea, he could do it without my help. I announced my intention to go and live on the boat until he was installed in his new flat when I would join him for the few weeks that must elapse before mine was ready.

I packed some freelance work and a few clothes and took myself off to Shepperton Marina where the boat was moored. The two Westies came too. There was no question about who was going to get custody of the dogs, they made their preference quite clear.

For ten lovely spring days I stayed on the boat. It was late April and the first warm spell in what was going to be a long, hot summer. The river birds were all busy with their young and for a neighbour I had a moorhen who had made her nest on the propeller shaft of the boat in the next mooring. She went on feeding her family, unconcerned by my presence. I worried in case someone came and started the engine before they were ready to leave.

John came to see me and took me to dinner in the pub. Softened by a little wine, he wondered aloud whether we were doing the right thing. I shook my head: 'I think we have reached the point of no return.'

He didn't argue, and he didn't charge me rent for the month I spent as his house guest, occupying a separate bedroom. Knowing our time together was coming to an end, we behaved as families sometimes do when a child is dying, packing the remaining days with pleasure.

He kept up his squash but found time to spend with me. We ate out and went to the theatre; John displaying his unbelievably lucky knack for finding parking spaces, some-times within yards of the entrance, and paying his usual attention to detail, buying chocolates and ordering drinks for the interval. Whenever we were both in central London, we would meet in Selfridges' ice-cream parlour and share one of their sundaes served in an enormous dish, with two spoons.

'I am going to change my car,' he said, on one such occasion. 'Do you want to take it over?'

'I couldn't run a car as big as that. I'd rather have a little hatchback, but I'm thinking of doing without a car and just hiring one when I want to go to Devon. It must be cheaper in the long run.'

A day or two later, he led me outside to see a small black Nissan. No pink ribbon, but a gleam of pleasure in his eyes as he handed it over. 'Because of all we've meant to each other,' he said, then, as if he'd read my thoughts, 'It's all paid for and taxed and insured for a year.'

Catherine called to see me, when she knew for certain that John would be out, struggling over from Twickenham with the infant on the bus. I gave her a lift home. She admired the new car. 'John and I are parting,' I told her, 'this is part of the deal.' She didn't answer for a moment.

'I'm amazed,' she said, 'I don't know what to say.'

When her reaction came, it was one of unconditional approval. Stephen too did not try to disguise his pleasure. 'Now you'll blossom,' he said.

'Or wither.'

In the course of my work for the nursing press, I had dealt many times with articles on the subject of bereavement. I knew that studies had shown it to be a roughly two-year process, the sufferer passing through several distinct stages from disbelief to anger, then grief and finally acceptance. 'Okay,' I reasoned with myself. 'You'll have to grit your teeth for two years, but then you'll be all right.'

I thought I had prepared myself pretty well, but the misery that engulfed me was like a physical weight. This wasn't exactly bereavement. In a way it was worse. When somebody dies, they have no choice but to leave. Rejection is harder to take and the recovery process much the same. As a dumped common-law wife, I received none of the sympathy and support that had been heaped on me as a widow, when in truth, I hadn't needed it. Perhaps I was getting my come-uppance.

John's nature would not allow him to be alone for long. I knew that, but I was shocked when I called at his flat in the afternoon a few days after I moved out, to find a woman there. I knew her, she was a friend of his from the squash club. I cursed myself for my stupidity. I should have phoned first; a mistake I would not make again.

They were neither of them in the least put out. She emerged from the kitchen I had so recently quit and offered me coffee. I accepted. As I drank it, I realised that of course, she was the reason for his many absences on so many weekends over the past two years. If there was a competition for gullibility, I'd be world champion.

I made his curtains as I had promised and he came round to fix shelves and towel rails for me. I remarked that it should be a condition for all separating couples that he gave her an electric drill and she gave him a sewing machine. Once the settling-in was done, I didn't contact him, but he phoned me almost every day. It was easy for him to make the transition to friendship. I tried, but for the one that still loves, it isn't possible, though I kept up the pretence.

I was listening to the *Today* programme on the radio before going off to a job, when I heard Rabbi Blue deliver the 'Thought for the day'. Mornings were difficult. I'd long been used to spending my evenings alone but waking in an other-wise empty bed to my own quiet orderliness was hard to bear. Blue was holding forth on the subject of divorce and separation, warning against bitterness. 'If you love someone, you must love them enough to let them go,' he counselled.

I was trying very hard, but a dragging depression was robbing my existence of all light and colour. Something had to be done. I ruled out Valium and enrolled on a kind of DIY counselling course, one of a whole series devised by a couple of American psychologists, who had tapped into a way of making money from people's emotional problems. It was the cheapest and shortest of the courses available, designed to enhance self-esteem. Mine badly needed a boost. It helped a lot. I discovered, in the course of guided self-analysis, that I felt I had already ceased to exist. Eunice had joined the company of the walking dead. This was clearly not the case and I began to feel a bit better.

John and his girlfriend went on a treasure-hunt trip to Paris that he had seen advertised in *The Times*. He phoned me on his mobile phone from the ferry. They needed help with one of the clues. I swallowed my resentment and consulted my encyclopedia.

The early days of bachelordom seemed to suit him. He got a woman in to clean and sent his shirts out to be laundered. Like me, he had never lived alone before and he was enjoying the freedom to come and go without having to offer explanations to anyone, but he couldn't stand his own company around the house and the new girlfriend was either not the live-in sort or, now that he was free from all encumbrances, pursuing her lost its appeal.

He turned up on my doorstep holding a tin of custard. He had in mind finishing off a blackberry and apple pie I had made for family lunch the day before. He confided his loneliness to me. 'You know,' he said, waving the dessert spoon, minuscule in his big fist, 'I'm no good on my own.'

'You hardly ever are alone,' I countered, mentioning his girlfriend. 'She is there with you most nights.'

'Yes, but she's got another regular boyfriend, and she's very sexy, but she's so boring.'

'Perhaps you need a circle of friends, at least until you find someone you can settle with. I hope you'll find someone who has no children; you're lousy with children. And watch out for AIDS.'

'I don't think I'm in any danger of that,' he said indignantly, 'I'm hardly promiscuous. Anyway, this friend of mine from the squash club, the one that has the water-skiing weekends, is in the same boat. We're going to go to one of these singles clubs.'

The experiment was moderately successful. He reported back. His friend had met someone he liked enough to invite out to dinner and John had taken a lady to the theatre.

'She was really very nice,' he told me. 'She had this super flat in Ealing. Nice skin and interesting to talk to. I was thinking she might do, but then she told me she was fifty.'

'But you're fifty-three.'

'I know, but I want someone at least ten years younger.'

'One day you'll get what you deserve,' I said. 'You'll fall for a dazzling blonde who'll dump you. You've certainly got it coming.'

His friend had encountered a similar problem. The women they were able to meet were just not in the right age range. John found a twenty-five-year-old willing to go out with him, but complained that it was like conversing with a fourth former.

'Why don't you just buy one of those inflatable women?' I asked. 'Then you could do all the talking.'

Failure made him quite despondent. He moved house again and decided to cut his overheads by working from home. This solved a problem for me. I'd been getting complaints from an elderly neighbour about Daisy, the brainless, good-natured one of my dogs, yapping while I was out of the house.

John suggested that I take them to him in the mornings, as he was at home most of the day, and collect them in the evening. I had a better idea. I took them on Sunday night and picked them up on Friday. He gave me a key so neither of us was tied down by the arrangement.

This latest of his moves proved lucky for him. He met the blonde of my prophecy. They were parking their respective cars and she stopped him to congratulate him on his charming son, who helped her when she had trouble with her starter motor. John asked her out to a wine bar for a drink and she invited him to join some other guests at a small dinner party.

She was a superb cook and an accomplished hostess. A huge international corporation employed her to entertain important clients and even the smallest, most informal gathering in her home was conducted with a professional polish.

John was in love again. He flopped on to my sofa, his eyes shining and told me how unbelievably lucky he was that someone so utterly beautiful and wonderful should condescend to take an interest in him. She was Roman Catholic which, he feared, might be a drawback. Otherwise, she was absolutely ideal, about forty-three, childless, a divorcee and had just moved to live opposite him in the block we had vacated (with a balcony overhanging the marina). Her kitchen window was visible from his lounge.

While his eyes were riveted to one side of her flat, mine were often on the other. Every day I walked the dogs along the spit of land that separated the marina from the open river. Looking at the boats and the activity on the balconies beyond, I suddenly saw John at her bedroom window. He was standing on something, a chair probably, obviously fixing a curtain rail in place. In a moment she appeared below him, holding out her hand, passing screws up to him. She turned her face up and he smiled down, the window framing a cameo of their pleasure in each other.

It wiped me out. I went home and lay on the couch, face to the wall, too paralysed to practise the exercise taught me at the self-esteem enhancement class, to examine my pain and breathe through it. I should have found a class that dealt with despicable, degrading, consuming jealousy.

Their love-making got off to a poor start. Impotence struck. He came to me, despairing. 'Don't worry,' I tried to be reassuring. 'If you remember you had this trouble once before, but you soon got over it. Once you stop thinking of her as some kind of royalty, it'll be all right, but don't forget, no one wants an apologetic lover.' I found him a couple of articles on the subject.

It crossed his mind that perhaps he'd gone too far in confiding that particular problem, that it might hurt me. Either he was quite incapable of putting himself in another person's shoes, or my performance as the completely collected woman, indifferent to his antics, was totally convincing.

Once, he invited me to his flat for a drink because his second son was visiting and had said he'd like to see me. I realised quite quickly that they were all going out to dinner later, with the new woman, and that I was expected to take my leave.

I made it to the door before the tears started to spill, but not before John had seen them. He handed me his perfectly laundered handkerchief and hurried me out without a word. Ordinary friendship, for me, was obviously not feasible. The sooner I stopped seeing him altogether, the better, but I had no doubt that contact between us would dwindle as his new relationship matured.

He stopped asking me out in the evening, but he always looked to see if my car was outside, an indication that I was perhaps working at home, and if it was, rang to see if I would like to go out to lunch. This was easier to cope with; we both had work to go back to and, for me, parting afterwards was less of a wrench. We got into a quite comical situation where he was keeping assignations with his 'ex' secret from his current love.

She knew we were still on friendly terms, because of the dogs. John called to collect them one Sunday, when they were planning a walk in Windsor Great Park. She waited in the car while he climbed the four flights of stairs to fetch them. I suggested she might like to come in for coffee but he turned the idea down, saying he didn't think either of them could handle it. I saw his point; though she had nothing to fear from me, he seemed to have appointed me to fill his mother's role.

He was besotted with her and admitted as much, though her religious beliefs were turning out to be a bit of a stumbling block. They prevented her from allowing him to spend every night with her and she had made it clear that on the forthcoming Christmas visit to see her mother and large family of older sisters, he would have to sleep on the sofa.

It was, it seemed, OK to sleep together so long as it wasn't openly acknowledged. I found it quite baffling. John explained that it had something to do with profound guilt at having divorced her husband, but it was something he couldn't understand himself. It clearly bothered him that he had come up against an unaccustomed resistance that he didn't know how to overcome.

'She's very devout,' he told me in awed amazement, 'I'm always coming across her praying and she's got little statues and crosses everywhere. She won't come and live with me.'

A warning bell sounded in my head. 'Listen. I hope you're going to tell her about the past, but if you can't, I promise you she won't hear it from me, unless you try to marry her without getting free of Pat. You try that and I'll go to her and tell her everything.'

He shrugged. 'It'll just be a formality after all this time. I just have to make an application to have her presumed dead.'

'You'd better do it then and I'd like to see the confirmation when it comes.'

How I'd carry out my threat, I didn't quite know. There was nothing to prevent him taking her off and going through a marriage ceremony without my knowing, but he obviously took me seriously. A few weeks later he told me a court hearing of his application to be freed from Pat had been fixed for September.

The Christmas visit was a great success. He made a hit with

her mother and the big sisters. He brought the snaps over to show me. There were shots of the festive table; the two of them on the snowy porch, arms wrapped tightly round each other; John dressed as Father Christmas and John presenting his gift to his beloved. It was a pretty white Austin Metro, sunshine roof, white-wall tyres, parked at the kerb, tied in a huge red bow.

The January sales were on. He went with her to Harrods. She bought all her clothes in Harrods' sales, which was why, he informed me, she dressed so well on an income no bigger than mine. He bought her a horrendously expensive dress, backless and with a handkerchief hemline, which had been reduced to being merely extremely expensive. She wore it to several New Year parties, drawing admiring looks from the men and envious ones from the women, according to John. She gave him a silver-topped hip flask to take with them to the golf course.

Golf was a love they shared, like their love of Cyprus. She and her husband had owned a villa in Kyrenia, in that part of the island annexed by the Turks. They were still awaiting compensation.

I resented her, of course. She had inherited everything I had chosen to discard; my lover, a home on the river. It was illogical; John and I had already parted when they met, so she was totally blameless, if blame can ever be attached to such events. Who was I to complain? He'd been married when he fell for me. The possible consequences of that piece of infidelity made me sweat to think about.

21

Déjà Vu

All through the summer the love affair ripened. She wore the sapphire engagement ring he slipped on her finger in the shadow of Nôtre Dame. They often went to Europe for weekend breaks and once to New York, to see *Phantom of the Opera* on Broadway. He filmed her skating on the rink at the Rockerfeller Center and walking in Central Park.

In the autumn they spent two weeks golfing in Portugal, driving across France in his sleek Japanese car. He called me when they got back. 'We had a marvellous time,' he said, 'but what terrible roads! And the drivers were even worse. It's almost a pleasure to get back on the North Circular. I've been in fear for my life.'

I made polite inquiries about the depth of his sun tan and the quality of the food. He reassured me on both points.

'By the way,' he said, 'I was in the Galley the other night. We came back on the Roscoff Ferry to Plymouth and I took her to Salcombe. We stayed with David Grose at the Thurlestone Hotel so we could get in a game of golf, but I took her to the Galley for dinner.'

He prattled on about the meal and the new owners. I couldn't believe what I was hearing. He knew Salcombe was sacred ground to me. How could he imagine I'd want to hear about him taking another woman to the town where I had stood in the pillory and sacrificed my good name for love of him? I wasn't just hypersentitive. The man was devoid of all feeling. How dare he advertise his contempt for me by flaunting his new mistress in front of my friends?

'What are you doing today?' his voice ran on pleasantly. 'Shall we go out for lunch?'

I needed to think. I like to keep my hot temper under control, to be sure my anger is justified, before saying things that might be difficult to retract.

'No thank you. I'm going to Ealing to do some shopping.'

From his point of view, it was reasonable to want to show his love the place where he'd spent eight years of his life. After all, I'd been taken to see almost every home he'd ever had, and they could be counted in dozens, the villa in Cyprus, the bungalow in Elstead, the barracks in Elgin. Still, I was seething, and not just about him taking her to Salcombe. I needed to off-load a lot of pent-up rage.

The doorbell rang. It was him again. He planted a kiss on my cheek. 'I'll run you to Ealing. We can have a bite to eat and I can take this back.' He held up a can of expensive aftershave. 'The atomiser button is jammed.'

We lunched in one of our old haunts in the beautiful new shopping precinct, then went to a large department store. John made his way to the men's cosmetics counter. I wandered about looking at clothes, and after a few minutes, I wandered back. He was still at the counter. There was a restrained argument going on.

'What's the matter?' I asked.

'I am waiting for the manager. This lady won't give me a replacement because I can't prove I bought it here.'

I waited with interest to hear what the manager had to say. His eyes travelled over John's height and width. That's that, I thought, he's taken a dislike to him. The manager listened carefully, then mustering the detached manner reserved for dealing with difficult customers, he sided with the salesgirl and refused to hand over a new can.

'I see,' said John. 'Will you excuse me a minute?'

He reached inside his jacket and took out his mobile

phone. The number of the company producing the after-shave was printed on the can. He dialled. 'Customer-relations department please.'

If I'd been phoning, they would have been out to lunch, or in a meeting, but he got straight through. There was a brief conversation.

'He would like to speak to you,' John said, holding out the receiver to the tight-lipped manager. A few minutes later we were leaving, with a replacement can of after-shave.

By now, the moment for giving vent to my anger had passed. On the way home, he inquired how I was getting on, whether I had found an interest to occupy my leisure time, whether I had met anyone else. I explained that for me, changing partners was a little more complicated than changing a dirty shirt. 'Anyway, I'm far too old. If every available man is looking for someone ten years younger, all I'm going to get is someone with a dodgy prostate.'

As he opened the car door for me outside my flat, I said, 'You do know what a bastard you are, don't you?'

'Oh yes,' he said, 'I know.'

It was the closest I could get to punching him.

The insult washed off him, but he rang me at work on Monday, very upset by what I considered little more than a playful dig. He had been out when I'd taken the dogs to his flat that morning. I let myself in and went to the kitchen to fill their water bowl. He still had the magnetic letters bought from the Early Learning Centre, stuck on his fridge. We had used them for leaving cryptic messages for each other like 'gone shop, back soon'. A message, obviously written by the beloved, read 'I love John'.

I sorted through the few remaining letters to see what I could make. 'So does he,' I spelt underneath. He hung up on me later when his fury reduced me to laughter.

Generally, things were going pretty well for me. Against the odds I'd got a well-paid job that took me into a favourite part of the city every day. I was beginning to actually prefer living on my own; the frequent coming and going of my children took the edge off my loneliness and I had made new friends.

Stephen now had a baby son, Charlie, Catherine was more settled and Lorna's little business venture, a picture library, was expanding into a large, respected enterprise. For the moment, I was happy about them.

At times lately John had been less than his usual buoyant self. No rift had opened exactly, but he and his love appeared to have hit a rough patch. Suggestions from him that they both sell their flats and invest in a joint property, where she could indulge her interest in interior design, had not been enthusiastically received.

'I don't know what she wants,' he said moodily. 'She's always saying she's fed up with her job. She could give it up. If she moved in with me, I could set her up in a little upholstery business or something.'

I said nothing.

He had admired a mohair sweater worn by a friend and had searched the shops to find one like it for her, without success. Knowing she was a good craftswoman, he hit on the idea of buying her the wool to make one. She had been seriously displeased and made him take it all back.

'Sometimes, I look at her and I think, she's not that beautiful.'

'Really?'

Again, I couldn't comment. I'd never seen her close up. Only caught glimpses of her as they passed in the car. When we did come face to face, it was in a surprising way, though when the secretary on the switchboard told me who was calling, I had been half expecting it.

'Hallo.' She gave me her name, only slightly hesitantly, as though she'd rehearsed what she was going to say. 'I'm John's girlfriend.'

'It's OK, I know who you are.'

'If you wouldn't mind, I'd like to talk to you.'

'I don't mind. Do you want to come to my flat, or shall I come over to you?'

'No. I don't want John to know about it. I'd suggest meeting somewhere after work, but I'll have to tell him I'm working late and he might ring. Could I ask you to come here, to my office?'

'All right.'

'You know where it is?'

'Yes. At least, I know where the building is.'

'I'll let the man on the gate know you're coming and he'll show you where I am.'

It was arranged for 8.30 the following evening.

Vanity obliged me to wash my hair and dress with particular care. I had to acknowledge that curiosity about to be satisfied only partly accounted for my anticipatory pleasure, the rest was down to the sweet scent of vengeance. I would have to keep myself in check; just answer her questions truthfully, give her only the information she asked for. I came up out of the tube into a cold drizzle and, warmed by sisterly charity, crossed the road to keep my appointment.

We had never met, but there was immediate recognition as she came forward to greet me. John was right. She wasn't exactly beautiful, but extremely glamorous. Blonde hair, well cut, reasonably slim, long legs, the skirt skimming the knees, high heels. I could see he would find her stunning. There was a flamboyance about her, an almost blatant statement of sexuality.

Her office was quite luxurious. Sandwiches and a pot of coffee waited on a low table beside a deep armchair. She waved me towards it and took another, opposite me. She looked troubled.

Disturbing rumours about John had reached her. A prominent woman member of the Brentwood Dock residents' committee had come to her with a newspaper cutting and the story of a murdered wife. Was it true? I explained as briefly as I could the circumstances surrounding the disappearance of Pat and the children and about the police investigation. I took care to include the bigamy.

She listened intently without interrupting until I'd finished. 'What do you think? Do you think he killed them?'

'I couldn't have lived with him for twelve years if I wasn't convinced he didn't do it.'

'How can you be so sure?'

'I can't be 100 per cent sure, but the police took the whole place apart and never found a scrap of evidence. And if you knew what Salcombe was like, you'd understand what I mean. He would have had to kill her one night and get rid of the body, the two children the next night, then get rid of them, all without leaving a trace and without being seen. It's only a little place, but it's like a big city. It never sleeps. As the pubs and restaurants close, fishermen are getting up to get to the fishing grounds. There's always someone about. He could never have done it. It just isn't feasible and anyway, you know what he's like, he isn't a violent man.'

I hoped she'd be reassured.

'You owned the Galley Restaurant, didn't you?'

'Well, it was actually left to my children. I had a life interest.'

'And was John's father's name Charles?'

'No. It was Jack. Why?'

'Well, we went there for dinner. He told me it had been his restaurant. He'd inherited it from his father whose name was Charles.'

'Charles was my husband. He died just before I met John.'

'He told me all about that mast in the ceiling. How it took ten men to get it into position.'

'That's true, but John wasn't there. I told him that story about Charles and some of the fishermen lifting it into place.'

'And he took me to see a house where his mother lived, where he grew up. A house in the country, near a beach.'

'No, he grew up in Bournemouth. That was our house, where my kids grew up.'

I was finding it difficult to swallow the sandwich. I couldn't finish my coffee.

'Did his mother have a villa in Majorca, in a mountain village?'

My hand was a bit unsteady as I put down the cup. 'Oh dear. No. That villa belongs to my daughter's agent. We had a couple of holidays there.'

'When I said I was concerned about the amount of money he's been spending on me, he told me his mother left him £100,000.'

I'd been a bit concerned about that too.

'It was closer to £20,000.'

I looked into her face. She gave no indication of whether she believed me. It didn't matter. There appeared to be nothing more she wanted to know and I got up to bring the interview to an end. I had expected she would offer to drive me home, since we were going to the same place, but she picked up her internal telephone and ordered a car to come to the door to pick me up.

She thanked me for coming and walked with me to the car.

'Will you be all right?' she asked through the window.

'I'll be fine. Will you?' She nodded and waved me off. A strong lady, faced with a decision as I had been, thirteen years before.

Deeply disturbed by the interview, I spent the night in a sweat of anxiety. Was John mad? All my careful rationalisation of his actions was crumbling, and that terrible doubt about his innocence of murder surfacing from where I'd had it comfortably buried for so many years.

If he could tell such massive, irrational lies, lies that would have to be sustained by other lies, for no reason other than to impress the woman he wanted and make her see him in a glamorous light, of what else might he be capable?

Could he have committed a series of unnecessary, premeditated murders, because he thought the victims stood between him and something he was determined to have? It was a possibility. For the first time I forced myself to admit that I might, however indirectly, have triggered the killing of a woman and her children. I didn't flatter myself that it might have been done for love of me, but I was the key by which he might gain a successful restaurant and the status and lifestyle that went with being its proprietor.

At work the next day, I seized the chance to talk to one of my senior colleagues, qualified in psychiatric nursing, when I found him alone in the smoking room. 'Andrew, how exactly do you define "psychopath"?'

My question didn't surprise him; he probably assumed it was something I'd come across in a manuscript that needed clarification. I had already looked it up in a medical dictionary and learned that it described an 'antisocial personality disorder', a kind of personality characterised by an inadequate set of moral and ethical standards; individuals with very little conscience.

His reply could have been lifted straight from the textbook. It helped, but didn't tell me what I really wanted to know. 'It doesn't mean someone who might run amok with an axe, commit murder, or go to any lengths for personal gain?'

'Not necessarily.'

'What about someone who tells elaborate, unnecessary lies? Lies that could easily be uncovered at any minute.'

'Could be a psychopath, or it might just be a not very nice person. There are such things as bad people.'

'Thanks.'

I brooded on the answer. Was John sick or evil, or neither?

No calls or invitations for lunch came in the next week, for which I was thankful. The mixture of pity and contempt I was feeling would make it difficult to face him; maybe I never wanted to see him again.

The call, when it came, was from her.

'I've decided I'm going to end it with John. I'm going to give him back all the things he's given me. I've asked him to come over on Saturday morning, but I want you to be there.'

'What?'

'He can't tell me any more lies if you're there and I'm a bit frightened.'

'You've no reason to be frightened. He won't hurt you.'

'When I told my sister about it she nearly went off her head.'

Obviously they had weighed the evidence of the past and brought in a guilty verdict. My own belief may have been badly shaken but I was still certain he wouldn't strangle anyone or bludgeon them over the head. It just wouldn't be his style and anyway, she was the thing he desired, not an obstacle between him and that thing, that he might seek to remove.

'He really won't hurt you.'

'You're very sure of that, aren't you?'

'Yes.'

'But I'd feel so much safer if you were there.'

'OK. I'll come.'

'Can you come early, to be sure of getting here before him?'

'What time?'

'10.30? He's coming at eleven.'

Nervous she may have been, but no other emotion showed as, sipping coffee, we discussed our feelings for the man who had had such an impact on both our lives and waited for his arrival.

'He always speaks affectionately of you,' she said. 'He did say you were perhaps a bit too close to your children. And he said you're not a very good cook.'

I never had been able to regard that sort of remark as a slight. He'd told me she was dyslexic and I knew which disability I'd rather have. I kept that to myself.

'Do you love him?' I asked, wanting to know what degree of sympathy might be appropriate.

'No, not really, but I liked him a lot. I prayed to St

Anthony to send me someone kind and I thought he'd answered my prayers.'

'He did. John is kind; you might have been very happy together.'

'Well, we couldn't be after this. To think I was about to give up my job and keep house for him. Thank God I didn't.'

She got up and went to a side-table.

'Look at this.' She handed me a legal-looking document. 'He said it was his divorce paper from Pat, but he's been altering it.' She pointed to one or two places where small patches had been painted out and inked over. 'It's his decree absolute from his first wife with the dates changed.'

It was beyond belief.

'What a fool.'

At eleven exactly, the fool in question rang the doorbell. I sat tight in my chair by the window as she ushered him in. His expression froze when he saw me. 'I asked Eunice to come,' she said from the doorway. 'I wanted her to hear what I have to say to you.'

He took the chair by the door without answering. After that initial glance when he'd taken in my presence, he didn't look my way again, nor did he speak directly to me. For the few minutes she was in the kitchen making him coffee we sat in silence. Handing him the mug, she wasted no more time.

'I have asked you here to tell you that I don't want to see you again,' she said firmly. 'I am returning everything you have given me. I've put them all out by the front door.'

'You don't need to do that,' he said. Shoulders hunched, he seemed almost to have shrunk physically.

'I must,' she countered, 'and I can't keep the car. It's much too expensive. Have you sold my other one?'

'Yes.'

'Well, you can replace it with something else, anything will do, if it's the equivalent of my old car.'

He came up with an answer immediately. 'I could let you

have Hilary's car.' Hilary was his assistant. The car was a Nissan, bought for the company; like mine, but older.

'Is it paid for?' she asked.

'Yes.'

'That'll do me. And you may as well take this with you.' She handed him the divorce papers. 'I can't imagine what you thought was the point of telling me all those lies about the restaurant and your life in Salcombe.' He fell silent, his eyes on her face like a reprimanded dog. It was pitiful.

'Was it,' I asked quite gently, 'to dazzle her?'

'Yes,' he said, not shifting his gaze, 'it was to dazzle her.'

'And you altered the dates on this paper, didn't you?' she demanded.

'Yes. Couldn't we talk about this on our own?'

'No. When you go, I don't want to see you again. You may not realise it, but Eunice is the best friend you've got.'

Still he didn't glance in my direction. 'I know that. Unfortunately, I don't want her and she knows it.'

He spoke the truth for once. I did know it. I felt nothing, no stab of pain, only numbness and a quiet marvelling at her efficiency. She'd given me an object lesson in how to end a damaging relationship. Too late for me to benefit.

He left quietly. I didn't move. She walked with him to the door. I heard the sound of objects being gathered together and the door close behind him. A minute passed. I imagined her leaning against the wall, breathing a sigh of relief. Now, I thought, she'll want to be rid of me, but she looked in and said: 'Let's have some more coffee.'

I followed her into the kitchen. We looked across the roadway to the window of his living room. No movement or light showed within.

'What do you suppose he's doing now?' she asked.

'He's probably sitting hunched in an armchair with his arms across his chest,' I answered.

'My God. I'm getting all the locks changed this afternoon. Aren't you afraid?'

'No. I know he won't hurt me.'

'Even after this?'

'No.'

Clearly she thought I was a fool, which, undeniably, I was, though not the kind to be mistaken about this. A fool only to be still weighed down by a sense of loss.

I didn't linger over coffee. Despite the bond that now existed between us, born of sharing an extraordinary experience, there was no room for pleasantries, no possibility of friendship. She came with me to the door and we parted as formally as if I had called to attend a committee meeting. Revulsion kept me away from him for the next five days or so then, when on my walks with the dogs, I saw that his car hadn't moved its position by an inch and no sign of life came from inside, I began to wonder if he'd done away with himself, concluding that he might have done everyone a favour if he had. My sense of responsibility reasserted itself and I phoned him.

'Are you all right?'

'Yes. I was going to come over to see you. I want to tell you something, but I don't want to discuss what happened the other day.'

'What would be the point?'

The weight loss in so short a time was staggering but in other respects he seemed as usual. As soon as he stepped inside, he said: 'I'm sorry I was rude to you.'

He was referring to the 'unfortunately I don't want her' remark. He knew that would be branded on my mind.

'Not rude, just unusually frank.'

'Well, I'm sorry. Sorry I can't be what you want me to be.'

'It really doesn't matter any more.'

'I won't be able to take the dogs for a few weeks. I'm going to France. With the Channel Tunnel coming, there'll be lots of English people wanting to buy property over there. I'm going to see about setting up an agency.'

'Fine.'

'If it works out, I'll go and live over there. I can't stay here. It's too close. Too many painful memories.'

'I know what you mean, but I thought things had been going wrong between you for quite a while. You said you were a bit disillusioned.'

'I only said that when I could see I was going to lose her. I was trying to prepare myself.'

With the end of our arrangement for the dogs, there was no reason for us ever to meet, except for the odd chance encounter in the shop or the street and they would finish when he moved away, but I was to see him once more.

Catherine had her second baby and I went to Twickenham to look after the family. She came home the day after the birth. From the bedroom window I saw him get out of a strange car.

'It's John,' I told her. 'May I ask him in?'

She nodded.

'Hallo,' he said breezily as I opened the door. 'What is it then?'

'It's a girl.'

Catherine joined us and we sat listening to how he had fared in France. There were definitely opportunities for the taking. He had stopped off on his way to Dover. He was going back to find somewhere permanent to live, then he was off for good.

He gave me a lift to the station car park where my son-in-law had taken my car that morning. I needed it to pick up the older child from school. The key had been hidden under the wheel arch. John waited until I signalled that I'd found it, then raised his hand in farewell, he found a gap in the traffic and accelerated across the road and out of sight. An ageing Prince Hal, off to conquer France.

22

Loose Ends

I'd been forewarned, so finding the young policeman at my door was no surprise. John's squash-playing girlfriend had told me to expect such a visit. She had been interviewed a few days earlier.

I had in any case already got wind of impending trouble for John, when the company owning the mobile telephone rang me to ask if I could tell them where he was. They were chasing overdue payment and were ringing all numbers used frequently by him, in an attempt to find him.

The police had the same mission, though the young man appeared bored and without hope, as he asked his questions. Beyond telling him John had gone to France, if that wasn't a lie, I couldn't help him much.

He was wanted for fraud. His lavish wooing had been financed from his client account, monies held during the conveyancing of property, by the solicitor or agent conducting the transaction, to be paid over on its comple-tion. Each time he helped himself, he had replaced the 'borrowing' from money paid in by the next client. No one suffered, until it came to the last unfortunate client.

'This poor family have lost their home,' said the policeman.

I was truly sorry.

'What about his flat? Can't that be sold to pay them?' I ventured.

'There's no equity left in that.'

'Is there any way they can be compensated?'

'Afraid not. If he gets in touch, you'll let me know?'

'Yes, I will, but I think it's very unlikely.'

John would have erased me from his memory by now, as easily as wiping the messages from the tape on his answering machine. I prayed that I wouldn't hear from him. Let me at least be spared having to turn him in.

In the following months the two girlfriends checked with me from time to time to see if I'd heard anything, but none of us had. It was a relief. In a curious way, hearing him say, 'I don't want her', had released me from an obligation to keep his secrets. I began to talk to a few close friends about the missing-persons inquiry, something I had until then found impossible. Gradually, the wish to set down what I knew of the disappearances grew in me.

It would be tricky, of course, from the point of view of libelling John, but he had done his own disappearing act and was no doubt living comfortably with another name and yet another woman. It would be unlikely to trouble him.

I considered whether revenge might be part of my motive, but couldn't say for sure; it didn't much matter. I concluded that the story was 'exceptional enough to justify the telling'. I set about gathering information and taking advice. I had just made a firm commitment to myself to go ahead when she of the squash club phoned: 'John's been caught. There's a report in the paper. He was tried at Kensington and sentenced to three years.'

'Are you sure it's him?'

'Yes. They got one or two details wrong, but I've checked. There's no doubt; he's definitely been sent to prison.'

'You don't know which one?'

'No.'

It would be easy enough to find out, I supposed, but after giving it some thought, I decided against writing to him or trying to see him. He wouldn't want to see me, or me to see him in humiliating circumstances. I phoned the other girl-friend and told her. She would be reassured to know he was behind bars.

I reflected on what difference this should make to my plans and decided not to be deflected. John would probably be free and out of sight again before any work of mine saw the light of day.

I wrote to the Chief Constable of Devon and Cornwall Constabulary, a successor to the one who had been in office at the time of the woman-hunt, telling him what I intended, asking if I could read my original statement and perhaps talk to the policemen who had been involved in the inquiry.

In reply, I received an acknowledgement from his personal assistant, followed a week or so later by a call from the deputy chief superintendent's secretary, saying he would like to see me. He was prepared to come to London to talk to me.

Coming up from Devon seemed a bit extreme; I rang back saying I intended to visit my mother in Salcombe soon, so why didn't we meet then? Confirmation came from an un-expected source. Dave, my friendly neighbourhood copper of so long ago, phoned to make the appointment. They would pick me up at my mother's flat, but on the day Dave turned up alone. The superintendent had been called to the Channel Islands to help in a murder inquiry, but hoped to see me another day.

An ability to forget faces totally has embarrassed me all my life, but I could be forgiven for not recognising Dave at once, even though I was expecting him. Luxuriant grey-black whiskers obliterated half his features, but as soon as he spoke, I knew him. I'm good at voices.

He greeted me and my mother warmly in his rich Devon burr. 'I couldn't believe it when the superintendent showed me your letter,' he said, 'I thought, well, fancy hearing from Eunice after all these years.'

After the obligatory tea, at his suggestion we took a stroll together, setting out along the creek road at an ambling pace.

Two old friends, but one a policeman possibly still not completely convinced of the other's innocence.

I went at once to what I thought must be the point of this visit: 'I don't know any more now than I could tell you at the time.' He heard me with a professional detachment, making no comment, so I tried again, to see if after all this time he might be prepared to express a personal opinion: 'Do you think John did it?' Then, receiving only a shrug in answer, 'Do you still think I might have had something to do with it?'

He would not be drawn, but turned to the subject of my writing about the inquiry. On that he was quite clear. He was opposed to the idea. 'Don't drag it all up again. You want to come back to live in the area, better to let it all be forgotten. Write about the Galley. That'd make a good story.'

Perhaps, but it didn't have quite the same compelling insistence to be told and unsolved mysteries never were forgotten.

He left me feeling uncertain whether I'd been hearing an official view, gently but circuitously delivered, or a piece of sincere advice from a friend.

The choice of venue for the postponed meeting was courteously left to me. Dave was a bit surprised when I proposed Kingsbridge Police Station, thinking I might find it upsetting, but it was convenient and an inconspicuous place to meet two policemen.

Oddly, the Detective Chief Superintendent reminded me strongly of John as he came into the room; not facially, but in stature and bearing. Another piece of type-casting, obviously. He was, every inch of him, the model of a charismatic chief constable in the making. He had, he told me, met me before, when he dined at the Galley one night before Charles died. I didn't remember.

I still didn't quite know why I was there, but began explaining the ideas behind my letter. 'I don't intend to try to solve the mystery, I wouldn't know how to start, or to question anything the police did. I am more interested in relationships. I'd like to show the effect the investigation had on the lives of me and my children, how a succession of strong, level-headed women could be attracted by a man like John. What it was about him that made Pat and me go on forgiving him?'

He listened attentively. 'I've no objection to that.'

Encouraged, I went on, telling him why I'd first felt serious misgivings about his innocence of murder; about the visit to the Galley with his new woman, the bizarre lies about his father's name and a boyhood in Salcombe. 'It made me wonder if he really is insane,' I finished.

'You do know where he is now?'

'I heard he was serving another three years in prison.'

'Yes. We picked him up in Ealing. Did you know he was calling himself Yabsley at the time?'

I almost laughed. How ridiculous to give yourself a distinctive name, connected with a scandal in which you were involved, when hiding from the police. He could as well have put a sign on his hat saying, 'Here I am, come and get me.'

'I didn't know it,' I said, 'but nothing he does can surprise me now.'

'Funnily enough,' the superintendent went on, 'I was feeding information about the case into the computer, a facility we didn't have at the time, when your letter arrived. I was looking to see if there was anything we might have missed or didn't tie up.'

'Will you let me read my statement? After fifteen years things have got a bit concertina'd in my mind. I'd like to refresh my memory and I'd like to talk to the sergeant.'

'The sergeant has retired because of his health. He's actually very sick, and you can't see your statement because we haven't closed the inquiry.'

I must have looked blank. I couldn't see how my reading what I had myself said could affect their inquiry. He explained that, at the time, it was thought that a charge of murder brought against John on the evidence then available was likely to result in an acquittal, after which it would be difficult, if not impossible, to bring him to trial. They had opted to wait. 'I know it isn't very likely after all this time,' he said patiently, 'but a new piece of evidence might just turn up and if he were to read something in a book of yours that might put him on the alert, it could jeopardise the whole case.'

It was disappointing, but there it was. I was going to have to rely on memory and what I could dig up from newspaper archives.

'There is just a remote chance,' I said, 'that if it's ever published and Pat is still around somewhere, she might read it and get in touch.'

'Yes,' said the superintendent, seeming to brighten, 'then that would finally remove the suspicion from John.'

At least he admitted that the possibility existed.

'If I can't read my statement, would you be willing to confirm or clarify points if I need it?'

'Yes,' he replied, but he sounded dubious.

'Give me a ring if you want anything,' said Dave on the way out. 'You've got my home number. Keep in touch.'

I thanked them and left.

Compiling a file of facts and dates to make a framework on which to build my work, I soon came up against two major problems: I couldn't remember exactly what John had said to me to explain why he lied about his mother coming from Bournemouth to collect the children after Pat walked out. What little I could recall seemed unacceptable to me now.

John must have been questioned on that point. I phoned Dave to ask him about it and about the oars that John said had been found sticking out of the car window. None of the newspapers had mentioned it, but John definitely told me the police had quizzed him about it.

Dave could either not remember or was not prepared to be forthcoming. 'You'll have to ask the superintendent,' he said.

So I wrote again to police headquarters explaining the problem and shortly received a polite note:

Dear Mrs Yabsley,
Thank you for your letter concerning the ALLEN affair. I am afraid the details you require are explanations given by ALLEN whilst he was being interviewed. As I explained when I last saw you, these matters remain confidential as the whole affair could be the subject of further inquiry. In view of that, I am afraid that I am unable to help you on the points raised.

Clearly, I was becoming a nuisance and was being politely but firmly dismissed.

Since Pat, Jonathan and Vicky vanished in 1975, I've thought of them often. Not every day, but often. After about ten years I began to think that perhaps one of the children, as they reached their late teens, might come in search of their father as their half-brothers had done, and so put an end to the mystery. I imagined a headline in the *Salcombe Gazette* saying 'John Allen Innocent', but life is never that tidy.

Some things I fear may come as a result of making my views of the affair public. That it may hurt some people; that I may myself be hurt. It may be that I shall have to answer for not revealing until now that John's arms were scratched on the morning after Pat left him, though whatever difficulties I have faced since the police hunt, I have been able to gather strength by telling myself: 'You survived that, you can survive this.'

Among the hopes is the perhaps not very realistic one that Pat or one of the children, now young adults if they are alive, may read this account and come forward. If not, if they truly are dead, with no stone to mark the place where they lie, no prayers having been said to mark their passing, let this be their memorial.

Warner now offers an exciting range of quality titles by both established and new authors. All of the books in this series are available from:

Little, Brown and Company (UK) Limited,
P.O. Box 11,
Falmouth,
Cornwall TR10 9EN.

Alternatively you may fax your order to the above address. Fax No. 0326 376423.

Payments can be made as follows: cheque, postal order (payable to Little, Brown and Company) or by credit cards, Visa/Access. Do not send cash or currency. UK customers and B.F.P.O. please allow £1.00 for postage and packing for the first book, plus 50p for the second book, plus 30p for each additional book up to a maximum charge of £3.00 (7 books plus).

Overseas customers including Ireland, please allow £2.00 for the first book plus £1.00 for the second book, plus 50p for each additional book.

NAME (Block Letters) ....

....

ADDRESS ....

....

....

☐ I enclose my remittance for _____

☐ I wish to pay by Access/Visa Card

Number ☐☐☐☐☐☐☐☐☐☐☐☐☐☐☐☐

Card Expiry Date ☐☐☐☐